GRACE KELLY STYLE

GRACE KELLY STYLE

H. Kristina Haugland

Edited by Jenny Lister
Designer Entries by Samantha Erin Safer

V&A Publishing

First published by V&A Publishing, 2010

V&A Publishing
Victoria and Albert Museum
South Kensington
London SW7 2RL

Distributed in North America by Harry N. Abrams, Inc., New York

ISBN 978 1 85177 599 6
Library of Congress Number 2009932296

10 9 8 7 6 5 4 3 2 1
2014 2013 2012 2011 2010

A catalogue record for this book is available from the British Library.

Designed by Schober Design
Copy-edited by Delia Gaze

Front jacket: Grace Kelly poses in an Oleg Cassini dress. Photograph by Erwin Blumenfeld
for *Cosmopolitan* magazine, April 1955.

Back jacket (left): Grace Kelly made even the most casual clothes look elegant, as shown in
this publicity photograph from *Rear Window* (1954).

Back jacket (middle): The bodice of Grace Kelly's wedding dress, designed by MGM's Helen
Rose, was made of antique lace and accented with tiny pearls. It suited the beautiful bride
perfectly (see p.44).

Back jacket (right): For formal occasions, Princess Grace wore spectacular couture dresses,
like this gown specially designed by Lanvin-Castillo to be worn with the sash, star and
badge of the Monégasque Order of St Charles (see also p.64).

Title page: This 1956 photograph by Yousuf Karsh illustrates the simple but regal glamour
of Princess Grace. Her evening gown and wrap are perfect foils for her pearl and diamond
jewellery by Van Cleef & Arpels, an engagement present from Prince Rainier.

Printed in China

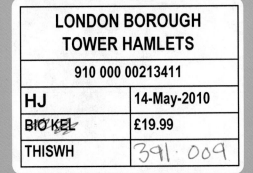

V&A Publishing
Victoria and Albert Museum
South Kensington
London SW7 2RL
www.vandabooks.com

Contents

The High Jewellery House of Van Cleef & Arpels, born of a marriage between Alfred Van Cleef and Estelle Arpels at the dawn of the twentieth century, is renowned for unparalleled craftsmanship and design. Using only the most exceptional gemstones, the House has come to symbolize both perfection and purity.

Van Cleef & Arpels has always played an important role in the great love story of Prince Rainier III of Monaco and Grace Kelly. In sponsoring this exhibition, we pay tribute to the timeless magic of Grace Kelly's iconic style, including Hollywood costumes and haute couture, and commemorate our connection with the Royal House of Monaco, which began with the exquisite diamond and pearl engagement set made for the princess in 1955, capturing the porcelain beauty of a 'fairy-tale' marriage, and continued with the House's appointment three months later as 'Official Supplier to the Principality of Monaco'.

Stanislas De Quercize
CEO and President

Van Cleef & Arpels

Princess Grace's 'Grande Marguerite' brooch, diamonds and sapphires set in platinum, by Van Cleef & Arpels, 1956.

03rd November, 2009

It gives me great pleasure to contribute to this celebration of the iconic sense of style possessed by my mother, Princess Grace.

As the photographs and text of this book show, she embodied the fashionable ideal of the 1950s, and became the ultimate beautiful bride when she married my father, Prince Rainier III. As Princess of Monaco, she exuded effortless elegance, whether she was appearing at the most spectacular official occasion, or a simple family gathering.

My mother treasured her clothes, and so made the accompanying exhibition possible. She loved to visit the United Kingdom, and had many friends there. She would have been delighted to have her dresses exhibited at the V&A.

Albert de Monaco

Introduction
Jenny Lister

Grace Kelly occupies a unique position in the history of film and fashion, epitomizing both the glamour of Hollywood and the allure of European royalty. With her classic, natural beauty, meticulous grooming and taste for simple, elegant clothes, her style was widely emulated and promoted as the 'Grace Kelly Look' at the height of her career in the mid-1950s. The actress's unfussy fashion sense shaped her image throughout the rest of her life.

As an actress, Grace Kelly was known for her utmost dedication to her work. The legendary costume designer Edith Head commented: 'She is the total professional in whatever she does, whether it is as model, actress or princess ... I have never worked with anybody who had a more intelligent grasp of what we were doing.'[1] In *Rear Window*, the mint-green suit worn by Grace Kelly's character is an exaggerated version of the neat, formal daywear the actress favoured at the height of her cinematic popularity in 1954 and 1955. By early 1956, when the 'fairy-tale' story of her forthcoming marriage to Prince Rainier III of Monaco so captured the public's imagination, young women in the United States and Europe — including Barbara Hulanicki, later the highly influential fashion designer of Biba in 1960s London — emulated Grace Kelly's image both off and on screen. In her memoirs, Hulanicki recalls how she copied Grace Kelly's blond, wavy hairstyle and searched the shops for an ice-pink twinset similar to one worn by the actress in *High Society*.[2]

Grace Kelly's costumes in *Rear Window* helped her to personify Hitchcock's vision of the sophisticated career woman with a strong sensual nature. Beneath her tailored jacket her demure blouse is actually a daring halter-neck top.

Prince Rainier and Princess Grace in the harbour of Monaco in 1963. Princess Grace's informal wardrobe included simple classic separates, given added interest here with a bold beaded necklace.

Grace Kelly's unpretentious attitude to fashion extended to her clothing decisions throughout her life, and her experience and technical understanding of costume design undoubtedly informed her fashion choices as a princess, when she was required to fulfil a very different role. The Hollywood costume designer Helen Rose designed regal and glamorous gowns for Grace Kelly's civil and religious marriage ceremonies, making use of the sumptuous materials and lavish attention to detail appropriate for a royal wedding that would be filmed and watched by fascinated audiences in cinemas and on televisions across the world. Her wedding dresses were, however, among the last American dresses the actress wore for public occasions. It was, of course, appropriate that, as Princess of Monaco, she should patronize the grand couture houses of France, such as Lanvin, Dior and Balenciaga, and adapt to the formality of court life.

As princess, Grace Kelly wore a different kind of costume — spectacular couture gowns accessorized by stately jewellery and Orders of Knighthood — with great dignity, as is plain to see in many exquisite portraits (see pp.64 and 72). Already a fan of the Christian Dior–New York label, the princess enlisted the help of Christian Dior himself to create the formal suits and sumptuous evening dresses she required for official visits abroad and society events. Dior's elegant solutions to dressing for formal occasions during her pregnancies were very successful, and confirmed the princess's lasting relationship with the house of Dior (see p.75).

The new Princess of Monaco found fresh outlets for her creativity, instigating cultural activities and an International Arts Festival, and reinvigorating the annual Red Cross Ball — events that required suitably eye-catching gowns. Marc Bohan became creative director of Christian Dior in 1960 and Princess Grace developed a friendly working relationship with the designer; by the late 1960s and throughout the 1970s she chose most of her evening wear from Bohan's Dior collections. As couturier to the princess, Bohan perfected the secret of designing for royalty, creating gowns that were 'totally conspicuous without being vulgar'.[3] Off-duty, Princess Grace continued to wear comfortable Chanel suits or shirtwaist dresses, a style she had helped to popularize in the 1950s. As her taste adapted to the changing fashions of the 1960s and '70s, her wardrobe evolved. Steering a course between the heights of hippy chic and severe restraint, Princess Grace also favoured classic fashions such as the timeless but ingenious draped jersey or sculptured taffeta creations of Madame Grès, gowns that were almost beyond fashion, and which suited her beauty and height (see p. 104).

Princess Grace's wardrobe not only reflects her refreshingly 'common sense' attitude to clothes but also the great stylistic changes that took place in the fashion world during the 1950s, '60s and '70s. From sophisticated ball gowns to meticulously tailored suits, her clothing reveals a personalized view of post-war couture and offers a rare opportunity to study the way a real woman — albeit one with a very high profile — approached the task of dressing for her public role.

Today, Princess Grace continues to be celebrated for her personal qualities and charitable work, as well as for her film career and her achievements in reviving the social and cultural life of Monaco. The influence of her personal style is still felt today, particularly each spring when the annual Academy Awards ceremony draws actresses to the red carpet. Though many emulate her style, few are able to achieve the poise and streamlined elegance of Grace Kelly — the actress, bride and princess.

Princess Grace, photographed by Lord Snowdon in the Winter Garden of the Princely Palace of Monaco for British *Vogue*, 1 March 1972. Her dress is by Marc Bohan of Christian Dior.

Grace Kelly Style

THE ACTRESS

By the time she was 11, Grace Kelly knew she wanted to be an actress. Although her goal was a serious stage career, she became a film actress and, in just a few years in Hollywood, made 11 films with top directors and actors, became a Hollywood star, and won numerous awards, including an Academy Award for best actress. During the same period, the young actress also came to be known for something apart from her beauty and talent: as a contemporary asserted, 'The thing that made her stand out is what we call "style".'[1]

Grace Patricia Kelly was born in Philadelphia on 12 November 1929 to John B. Kelly and Margaret Majer Kelly. Her father, the son of Irish immigrants, had founded the construction company Kelly for Brickwork, making him a millionaire; he had also won gold medals in sculling at the Olympics of 1920 and 1924, and later became active in local politics and civic concerns. Her mother, from a German Lutheran family, had converted to Catholicism on her marriage and was a former physical education teacher. In a large house — built of Kelly brick — in the comfortable East Falls section of Philadelphia, young Grace was brought up with two sisters and a brother. While she later demonstrated the familial values of hard work, thrift and self-reliance, as a child Grace Kelly stood out in a family of extroverted athletes. Shy and with delicate health, she made up little plays with her dolls, took part in amateur theatricals and was inspired by the stories of Broadway told by her uncle, the playwright George Kelly. She soon developed the ambition of becoming an actress.

With the drive and determination characteristic of her family, Grace Kelly set about pursuing her dream. In 1947 she convinced her parents to let her study acting at the American Academy of Dramatic Arts in New York. After graduating in 1949, she landed a part on Broadway in August Strindberg's play *The Father*, which starred Raymond Massey and ran for three months. She continued to take private acting lessons and appeared in numerous television plays and on stage in summer theatre companies and other theatrical productions. Her height, at 5 feet 6½ inches, was a handicap in obtaining acting jobs, and she often had to audition in stocking feet, but her tall, slim figure, combined with her 'girl-next-door' beauty, was perfect for modelling. As a student and fledgling actress, she was able to support herself by promoting products ranging from gowns to beer to insect spray, and her wholesome, fresh face appeared on a number of magazine covers.

The young Grace Kelly went to Hollywood in 1950 to appear in her first film, in the small part of a woman contemplating divorce in Twentieth Century Fox's *Fourteen Hours*; the following year she played the youthful Quaker bride of Gary Cooper's stoic marshal in the United Artists' western *High Noon*. She was offered contracts by several film studios, but she was not interested since her goal was to become a serious stage actress. In the autumn of 1952, however, she was offered an opportunity too good to reject. With the condition that she be allowed to continue her theatrical career, the 22-year-old signed a seven-year contract with Metro-Goldwyn-Mayer (MGM), Hollywood's largest movie studio, and set off to film *Mogambo* on location in Africa. Directed by John Ford, the film starred Clark Gable as a big-game hunter who dallies with both a showgirl (Ava Gardner)

Previous page. Philippe Halsman photographed Grace Kelly for the cover of *Life* magazine, 11 April 1955. Grace Kelly had worn this Edith Head-designed dress to the premiere of *The Country Girl* in December 1954 and to the Academy Awards ceremony on 30 March 1955.

Left. In 1947 Grace Kelly moved to New York to study acting at the American Academy of Dramatic Arts. Although she auditioned for several film roles after graduation, her main goal was to be a successful actress on the stage.

and a reserved, married Englishwoman played by the newcomer. *Mogambo* was a box-office hit when it was released in October 1953, and marked the start of Grace Kelly's rapid rise in Hollywood, earning her a surprise nomination for an Academy Award for best supporting actress.

By the time this nomination was announced, others were already discovering Grace Kelly's potential as an actress. In the late summer of 1953 MGM lent her to Warner Brothers for Alfred Hitchcock's *Dial M for Murder*, in which she portrayed an English wife whose husband (Ray Milland) tries to have her murdered. This was the start of a mutually beneficial working relationship with the renowned director. Hitchcock mentored the young actress, helping to mould her image, teaching her about filmmaking and, she later recalled, giving her confidence in herself. The director, in turn, was entranced with Grace Kelly's beauty and talent, and with what he called her 'sexual elegance', and believed he had found his ideal leading lady. He cast her in his next two films, for, as he told a reporter, 'She'll be different in every movie she makes. Not because of makeup or clothes but because she plays a character from the inside out. There's no one like her in Hollywood.'[2]

Grace Kelly was also starting to learn how much the nuances of clothing and appearance could add to a film. Except for a red lace dress by the costume designer Moss Mabry, her wardrobe for *Dial M for Murder* was all bought off the peg, but

Hitchcock nevertheless closely supervised the actress's look, ensuring that her clothes went from bright to sombre as her character changed. In one crucial instance, however, the perfectionist director's vision gave way to the actress's practical approach to clothing and her feeling of what was right for the character: while he had envisioned her wearing a velvet robe during the attempted murder, Grace Kelly insisted that it was more natural to wear only a nightgown to get up to answer the telephone. Impressed with her instincts, Hitchcock gave the actress more say in her wardrobe on their next films, which also used the skills of Paramount's chief costume designer, Edith Head. Known for her restrained designs, Head by this time had nearly 30 years of costume experience and had won several Academy Awards; she also had the ability to work well with both Hitchcock and his new star.

By late 1953 the trio was at work on *Rear Window*, the story of a photographer, played by James (Jimmy) Stewart, who is confined to his apartment by a broken leg and suspects his neighbour of murder. His romantic interest, Grace Kelly's character, is a beautiful and chic woman who works in the fashion industry and, as her boyfriend ruefully remarks, never wears the same dress twice. Hitchcock again dictated the colour and style of the actress's wardrobe for every scene, giving her clothes a vital role in advancing the conflict and action of the plot. Edith Head designed glamorous short evening dresses, an impeccably tailored suit, a sheer negligee and sleek nightgown, a full-skirted floral dress and casual jeans that helped to establish the dimensions and inner passion of Grace Kelly's character, a woman very much in love. During the filming of *Rear Window*, the designer and the actress became good friends, and even conspired to resist Hitchcock's directive that the star add 'something' to her bosom under the nightgown. Edith Head also discovered that Grace Kelly knew how to wear clothes; she later stated: 'Few actresses could have carried off the look the way Grace did.'[3]

Right. In 1953 Alfred Hitchcock cast Grace Kelly in *Dial M for Murder*. Her film wardrobe reflected her character's decline from an attractive wife to a prison inmate falsely accused of murder. The wardrobe test for Warner Brothers shows her in an alluring bright red lace strapless dress and bolero jacket.

Below. In *Rear Window*, clothes are vital to the definition and development of Grace Kelly's character and the action of the film. Edith Head designed this full-skirted, black and white evening dress for the dramatic entrance of Grace Kelly's character, who works in the fashion industry.

Edith Head again dressed Grace Kelly in early 1954 for Paramount's *The Bridges at Toko-Ri*. Based on James Michener's story, the film starred William Holden as a Korean War fighter pilot, and as his wife Grace Kelly's upper-middle-class clothes were relatively unexciting. The next two films that the designer and actress made together, however, showed the versatility and talents of both women.

In early 1954 Grace Kelly fought hard to get a much-coveted role in Paramount's *The Country Girl*, that of the bitter, dowdy wife of a washed-up alcoholic, played by Bing Crosby. Once cast, she set about convincing MGM to release her temporarily from her contract, and then transformed herself for her first gritty role. Edith Head and Grace Kelly worked together to create a wardrobe of unflattering housedresses and shapeless cardigans to help the actress become a drab, depressed wife. Once she looked and felt right for the part, she could concentrate on her acting, which received widespread acclaim.

Her next film, *To Catch a Thief*, directed by Hitchcock, was filmed on the French Riviera in the early summer of 1954. Grace Kelly, playing a self-assured heiress who beguiles a dashing former cat burglar (Cary Grant), was hailed as 'one of the most gorgeous creatures ever to be projected upon a theatre screen'.[4] Her alluring and luxurious clothes included striking beachwear, chiffon evening dresses, a peach day dress with chiffon scarf and a spectacular gold costume-ball ensemble. The studio took the unusual step of sending Edith Head on location, which gave the designer and star a chance to go shopping for accessories at Hermès in Paris, feeling, Head later said, 'like two girls in an ice-cream shop'.[5] The film was a visual delight,

Right. The south of France setting was intrinsic to the glamour of *To Catch a Thief*, filmed in 1954. Edith Head's costumes for Grace Kelly included this feminine ensemble worn for a scenic drive with Cary Grant, when her allure and the chemistry between them are obvious.

Right. Paramount sent Edith Head on location for the filming of *To Catch a Thief*; en route, the costume designer and Grace Kelly went shopping in Paris, where the actress indulged her weakness for buying gloves at Hermès to such an extent that she had to send for more money.

Left. The denouement of *To Catch a Thief* takes place during an extravagant masquerade ball. Edith Head, following Hitchcock's instructions, made Grace Kelly look like a princess, covering her in gold, with a hooped, strapless dress, matching wig and long gloves.

making the most of the spectacular Côte d'Azur settings and of Edith Head's beautiful costumes; even the extras in the film were meticulously dressed, and the film earned the designer an Academy Award nomination.

Grace Kelly also had a close relationship with another experienced, Academy-Award-winning costume designer, Helen Rose, MGM's chief designer. The studio was known for its glossy visual style, and Helen Rose's understated but up-to-the-minute designs perfectly suited both MGM and Grace Kelly. Helen Rose had costumed *Mogambo*, the actress's first film for MGM, but its safari-style wardrobe was not in the least glamorous (see p.38). The two also worked together on Grace Kelly's next MGM movie, *Green Fire*, filmed in Colombia in the spring of 1954, but the film — with Grace Kelly as a coffee-plantation owner opposite Stewart Granger's emerald hunter — once again had little sartorial interest.

Helen Rose had more creative scope in her next two films with Grace Kelly. *The Swan*, shot in the autumn of 1955, gave the actress lead billing as a young

Ruritanian princess who is courted by a crown prince (Alec Guinness) and a handsome tutor (Louis Jourdan) and learns to put duty before love. Given the rare opportunity to design period costumes, Helen Rose thoroughly enjoyed dressing the star for every royal occasion, creating 1910-style outfits for riding, fencing, negligee and evening. Publicity about the actress's white, high-waisted dresses and soft hairstyle started fashion trends even before the film was released in April 1956 (see p.38). By then, Grace Kelly's role in *The Swan* had become famous for another reason. Once her engagement to Prince Rainier III of Monaco was announced,

Right. In this scene from *High Society*, Tracy Lord, having drunk a little too much champagne, dances with journalist Mike Connor (Frank Sinatra), and has second thoughts about her wedding the next day.

it was considered a fascinating coincidence that the on-screen princess would become one in real life.

The filming of *High Society*, Grace Kelly's final film, took place in early 1956 amidst the storm of attention that surrounded her engagement. For this musical remake of *The Philadelphia Story*, she portrayed an aloof and aristocratic young woman, divorced from her first husband (Bing Crosby), who is about to remarry. For this high-budget film, set in the summer at the exclusive resort of Newport, Rhode Island, the designer, Helen Rose, created what she later called 'a complete daytime to evening collection of modern fashion',[6] including a Grecian-style bathing suit and wrap, a striped day dress, a chiffon ball gown and a wedding ensemble of a full-skirted dress of embroidered white organdie and a large-brimmed hat. During the filming of *High Society*, Helen Rose and Grace Kelly also conferred about the designer's most famous costumes for the actress — the civil and religious wedding dresses for her forthcoming marriage ceremonies in Monaco.

Left. A detail of the bodice of the *High Society* evening gown, designed by Helen Rose, showing the layers of grey and pink chiffon, embroidered with diamanté stones and silk thread. MGM studios gave the actress all her costumes from *High Society* for her trousseau, and she wore this dress on several occasions afterwards.

Right. *Screen Stars*, May 1955. Grace Kelly appeared on many magazine covers and was the subject of numerous articles in the mid-1950s, but she was famously discreet about revealing personal information.

Grace Kelly's rise to stardom had been sudden and spectacular. In January 1954 one Hollywood commentator noted that this was not hard to understand: '1. She is blonde and beautiful. 2. She can act.'[7] In April *Life* magazine featured her on its cover with the tagline 'Hollywood's Brightest and Busiest New Star' and made the prediction that 1954 would become 'this year of Grace'.[8] The accolades continued throughout the year: *Newsweek* hailed her in May as 'the latest star to reach Hollywood's top rung', while in November a United Press columnist echoed the general consensus in declaring her 'the most outstanding new star and hottest property of the year'.[9]

In early 1955 the acclaim for Grace Kelly took the form of awards for her acting abilities. In January she received the New York Film Critics Circle Award for best actress of 1954. In February she won the Hollywood Foreign Press Association's Golden Globe Award and was nominated for an Academy Award for best actress for her work in *The Country Girl*. She received this prestigious award in March; accepting tearfully and with thanks, she noted that the thrill of the moment prevented her from saying what she really felt. Grace Kelly's critical success was mirrored by her popularity with audiences: at the end of 1955 an annual ranking of the highest-earning stars proclaimed her — the only newcomer on the list — as the top female that year, second overall only to James Stewart.

Throughout 1954 and 1955, while the new star was heralded for her beauty and talent, there was also much discussion of her figure, manner and style. In all these categories, it was generally agreed, Grace Kelly was something startlingly different. At a time when voluptuous screen sirens, such as Marilyn Monroe and Gina Lollobrigida, and shapely 'sweater girls' were the norm, Grace Kelly's 'young Diana figure' set her apart.[10] While some authorities declared that she had perfect proportions, others were more critical. Edith Head was quoted as saying that she was perhaps a little too short-waisted and long-legged and had 'a waist that was much too small'.[11] She joined others, however, in praising Grace Kelly's posture, a feature that the actress had worked to improve after she first saw herself on the screen. Her greatest beauty problem, the star revealed, was keeping her weight

Left. This ingenious Grecian-style bathing robe, with a matching bathing suit, was worn by Grace Kelly for a scene in *High Society* by the swimming pool. The white, classical style set off the aloofness and goddess-like perfection of her character's personality.

down, which she did by riding, swimming and playing tennis when possible and by dieting occasionally.[12] Her discipline worked, for she took a size 10 dress, then the smallest size usually sold.

Grace Kelly, unlike publicity-hungry stars, was reticent about sharing personal details. At a time when an actress's measurements were considered 'standard data', she flatly refused to divulge hers. Although the press delighted in linking her name romantically to her co-stars and other men, she would not discuss her private life or even allow publicity photographs to be taken in her small Manhattan apartment. Her dignified, patrician air set her apart — even notoriously unceremonious press agents called her 'Miss Kelly'. *Vogue*, although claiming she was 'too wholesome to be mysterious', labelled her as 'remote as a Snow Queen'.[13] Reviews of Grace Kelly's on-screen performances and her personal publicity used certain words again and again: patrician, thoroughbred, genteel, reserved, cool, elegant and lady. This last descriptor was considered by many to sum up the essence of Grace Kelly — *Vogue* noted that it was 'the one phrase that pegs her'.[14] In January 1955 her appearance on *Time*'s cover emphasized this unusual aspect of the star with the caption 'Gentlemen prefer ladies'.

One particular clothing accessory was singled out as perhaps the most distinctive feature of the new star's 'unshow-businesslike quality'. In an attempt to distil Grace Kelly's character into five words, *Time* entitled their article 'The Girl in White Gloves'.[15] At the time, white gloves were commonly worn by well-bred girls and women, following the dictates of arbiters of etiquette such as Emily Post, who decreed that women should always wear gloves in church, on city streets, in a restaurant or theatre, and to go to lunch, a formal dinner or a dance. White gloves, prim and noticeable, were not common in Hollywood studios, however: the film director Fred Zinnemann remembered how Grace Kelly's appearance had startled him four years earlier: 'Nobody came to see me before wearing white gloves.'[16]

Kelly herself was perplexed by the focus on her ladylike qualities and unique-ness. Yet to many in the 1950s, when great emphasis was placed on proper feminine behaviour and the cultivation of a pleasing appearance, her unusual status as both a lady and a Hollywood star was refreshing and admirable. Her appeal did not rely on 'too blatant curves, too tight dresses, too lavish furs, or jewellery noteworthy only for its abundance', but on ladylike good taste.[17] Oleg Cassini, her on-and-off romantic interest in late 1954 and 1955, explained how this look worked for her: 'By wearing clothes that don't get too much notice, she gets noticed more herself.'[18]

The actress's personal style reflected her upbringing and wish to be taken seri-ously. She wore sensible and sedate clothing — shirtwaist dresses, understated but beautiful evening gowns, well-cut tweed suits, hats with little veils and low-heeled shoes — and made no secret of the horn-rimmed spectacles she needed for near-sightedness. Grace Kelly was also the perfect representative of the 'College Girl Look', a classic style that, commentators noted at the time, had a long history but had received little attention until the famous actress gave it prominence. This style was also known as the 'American Look', since the simple, uncluttered clothes and good grooming it promoted were said to fit perfectly the casual, unaffected way of life that was typical in the United States.[19]

Grace Kelly with her poodle Oliver, photographed by Erwin Blumenfeld, for *Cosmopolitan* magazine, April 1955. Through images such as this, the actress helped promote the 'College Girl Look' — a casual yet well-groomed style that was seen as typically American.

Grace Kelly credited her early modelling experience with making her aware of how she looked to others and teaching her about grooming and how to find the right clothing and hairstyles for herself. 'You can't be photographed by clever men without learning your good and bad points', she noted.[20] Having discovered that she looked best with her hair pulled back off her face and with very little make-up and light lipstick, she had the self-confidence to maintain this look even in Hollywood, saying: 'I had to follow what I knew was right for me.'[21] As an actress, Grace Kelly worked with skilled costume designers, directors, lighting artists, hairdressers and make-up artists, yet she was 'as matter-of-fact about beauty as she is about her fabulous rise to fame', and readily admitted that she did her own hair and nails off screen.[22]

She understood clothes and knew what suited her. 'I have to choose simple clothes', she explained, 'because when I wear anything dramatic I seem to get lost. In fact nothing very fussy is becoming to me.'[23] Edith Head named Grace Kelly in 1955 as one of only five movie stars she would trust in front of a mirror as judges of their own clothes. The actress's ability to wear clothes well also impressed observers; as Helen Rose attested, 'you know she will wear anything beautifully'.[24] Her excellent posture, innate poise and good grooming meant that the most casual clothes never looked sloppy on her; she could look elegant, it was said, 'even in

a skirt and an oversized sweater'.[25] She summed up her common-sense approach to her wardrobe by saying: 'I just buy clothes when they take my eye, and I wear them for years.'[26] While she liked purchasing new clothes, buying ready-made size 10s wherever she happened to be, her shopping was on a very modest scale because she became fond of her old things and felt comfortable in them. She noted that she still had clothes she had worn at school, and thought of herself as 'loyal to her old clothes, just the way she is loyal to old friends'.[27]

Her practical and distinctive approach to clothing was perfectly expressed by the icey blue-green satin ensemble she

During her early acting career Grace Kelly was also a very successful model. The experience of working with photographers taught her how to emphasize her best features; her height, posture and good grooming stood her in good stead in her acting career.

Grace Kelly at the Cannes Film Festival in May 1955. The actress's ladylike style and especially her predilection for wearing immaculate white gloves stood out amongst other women in the film industry.

elected to wear to the Academy Awards ceremony in March 1955. Designed by Edith Head, the ensemble — a slim, draped sheath gown with back drapery and a matching floor-length evening coat — was a favourite. She had already worn it to the premiere of *The Country Girl* in December 1954, and also posed in the gown — with an added fold of fabric across the bodice top — for the photographer Philippe Halsman, as shown on the cover of *Life* magazine on 11 April 1955 (see p.12). The bustle-back

Above. On 30 March 1955 Grace Kelly received an Academy Award for her performance in *The Country Girl*. She wore a favourite dress, designed by Edith Head, with a matching full-length evening coat, a needlepoint bag by French luxury label Morabito and a soft chignon hairstyle.

Left. A detail showing the flattering silhouette of the Edith Head satin dress that Grace Kelly wore at the Academy Awards ceremony; the slim skirt with drapery swept into a bustle at the back contrasted with the full-skirted dresses worn by other actresses at the ceremony.

dress and matching coat were appropriate and becoming, but since many stars at that year's Academy Awards wore full-skirted gowns topped with furs, Grace Kelly's unusual choice stood out and was seen as reflecting her famously 'different' nature. Press accounts described her long white gloves, pearl-drop earrings and soft upswept hairstyle accented with two yellow roses, and also recorded another characteristic feature of her appearance: she had dropped her horn-rimmed glasses in her excitement at winning the award.

Avoiding both extravagant purchases and flashy styles, Grace Kelly soon became renowned for what was termed 'conspicuous good taste'.[28] In late 1954 her classic, feminine style was publicly recognized when she was named on that year's Best-Dressed List, which tallied the votes of more than a thousand fashion editors and other experts to select ten prominent well-dressed women. Modelled after the original Parisian list, the Best-Dressed List was started in 1940 by the fashion publicist and arbiter Eleanor Lambert. Originally a publicity stunt to promote the New York Dress Institute, by the mid-1950s it had become both an annual news story and a respected barometer of style. Those who appeared on the list in the 1940s and early 1950s included royalty,

socialites and heiresses, established actresses, influential women, and those married to men of power and wealth. Grace Kelly's debut on the list was at a time when those named were still ranked in order; she was at the bottom, tied with Queen Frederica of Greece, while Mrs William Paley and the Duchess of Windsor tied for top honours.

As Grace Kelly's career blossomed throughout 1955, she also cemented her place as fashion leader. She was placed on the list of the Ten Best-Tailored Women by the Custom Tailors Guild of America, and the Dallas-based luxury department store

Grace Kelly Tells Ho

In the course of the last year or so, Grace Kelly has been boarding plane after plane to take her to Hollywood, back to New York, to South America, Europe, Africa. She has learned to concentrate on the clothes she needs most, to make good use of separates, dresses with jackets, sweaters. We show here the basics she considers most essential; she adds others according to the trip. "When I buy a suit for travel," she explains, "I buy one with some width in the skirt, so that it doesn't sit out on the plane. I like an evening dress that folds easily, doesn't need petticoats. I have a sleeveless black linen that I can wear on the street with a sweater or jacket, or dress up with jewelry for cocktails . . . cashmere sweaters take up little room or weight . . . a wide black skirt can be worn with a silk shirt or a scoop-necked sweater. I develop my travel wardrobe around black, use black shoes and bag with all daytime clothes."

There are seven musts for every woman who travels—to these you'll add some favorites of your own.

1. A topcoat: in such fabrics as tweed or flannel, it can go from city to country. In a neutral color or a mixture, it's slow to show dust and dirt.

2. A suit that co-ordinates well with the coat.

3. A second suit, or a skirt that matches or co-ordinates with the coat and one or two sweaters or tops to go with it (this is even more comfortable than a suit for long sessions on train or plane).

4. A short evening dress with a jacket that turns it into an afternoon dress. According to where you're going, keep this in a dark color or have a pretty light fabric, printed or plain—whatever you choose be sure it has a crease-resistant finish. Unless you go to formal parties, you won't need a long dress.

5. A simple dress to wear on the street or for after noon. Miss Kelly chose black linen—you might pre fer an easily washed synthetic.

6. A wrap for late afternoon and evening—fur, sill or simply a decorated sweater or stole—or solve th question with a silk or velveteen raincoat; otherwise add a light plastic raincoat to your "musts."

7. A supply of quickly washed and dried underwear at least six pairs of nylon stockings and a small dress hat or veil for afternoon.

The things that weigh the most—you'll need two pair of shoes with comfortable heels—if you try to use on pair for all your walking your feet will get twice a tired. One pair of pretty sandals can double fo afternoon and evening. You'll need a big handba and a small bag for dress. Make a careful check lis of cosmetics; watch the weight of your jewelry too

BY ELIZABETH MADEIRA and ROSELLEN CALLAHAN

RICHARD AVEDON

The dress with a jacket—wonderful for travel, because it's two things in one—a short evening dress or a cocktail dress. Made in peau de soie, weight 2¼ pounds. In black, it's timeless, can be varied with good accessories. Harvey Berin.

A sleeveless linen dress shown here as she would wear it by day, with a geranium cashmere sweater, collared in green silk. The sweater would look well over white, gray, pink, dull blue—any number of colors; the dress weighs 1½ pounds, sweater 1 pound. Both from Clarepotter. Coin necklace from Macy's Coin Center.

The travel coat and suit—herringbone tweed, arro straight, over a yarn-dyed worsted suit with easy ski Both from Ben Zuckerman. She'll board the plane these so it's not necessary to weigh them. The coat go over everything in wardrobe except her evening dre

Travel Light

You can travel light and travel right overseas with two pieces of luggage and a tote bag which doubles as a handbag. Minimum luggage avoids excess baggage charges and you can carry it yourself in a pinch. On domestic flights your free luggage allowance is 40 pounds; on international first-class flights, 66 pounds; on international tourist flights, 44 pounds. New ultra-light air luggage is roomy, very strong. The pieces we planned for this wardrobe are two 26-inch Pullman cases, total weight empty, 18 pounds 10 ounces. A plastic-lined cosmetic kit—plus 42 grooming items—weighed exactly 5 pounds. Clothes pictured here (without coat and suit) total 12 pounds 9 ounces. Lingerie, shoes, accessories weighed 6 pounds 8 ounces. Total: 42 pounds 11 ounces. This allows you a leeway of 1 pound 5 ounces, for little personal extras which nobody can foresee for you and which you would weigh for yourself.

Everyone knows by this time that

Grace Kelly is a lady blessed not only

with beauty and a very great talent for acting

but with most uncommon common sense.

When she packs to travel she makes

a list, pares her wardrobe to a minimum,

winds up with all the things she needs—

nothing that she doesn't wear

If she goes to the country she'll wear these twin sweaters with matching skirt, the blue will look wonderful with her tweed coat. Grace Kelly also has a sweater and skirt in dark gray to alternate with her suit for travel. Hadley sweaters, Sloat skirt. Both sweaters weigh 21 ounces, the skirt 2 pounds. Earrings are from Mazur.

The beautiful packable evening dress—rose-pink chiffon, very Greek in feeling. It has its own satin jacket (not shown). She carries a chinchilla bolero, charming too over an afternoon dress or dark street dress. Dress by Nettie Rosenstein, fur bolero from Ritter Brothers. Dress weighs 2 pounds, fur bolero 2½ pounds.

Neiman Marcus presented their award to the actress in recognition of 'her personal taste, elegance, and restraint in her personal clothing'.[29] Department store windows featured the image of Grace Kelly: in the autumn of 1955 Mary Brosnan Studios of New York, the leading American mannequin designer that sold to stores throughout the United States and Europe, used her likeness to create a line of mannequins. Grace Kelly's fashion influence was so pervasive that it affected others in Hollywood. In November 1955 a commentator noted: 'Ever since she came along other stars have gone all out trying to achieve that look of stylish simplicity.'[30]

The actress's assured but understated style — now named the 'Grace Kelly Look' — was accorded official status in the fashion world on 8 December 1955 in a short article in the retailing newspaper *Women's Wear Daily*, which hailed her as having 'a fresh type of natural glamour that personifies a typically American look'. Her look was said to have brought fresh attention and special prominence to a long-ignored style and to classic clothes — 'the easy shirtwaist dress, the carefully detailed tweed suit, the chiffon evening dress'. The actress, it stated, provided an excellent fashion model for teenagers, since 'she illustrates how to be casual without flying shirttails, how to be formal without looking bizarre'. These tasteful and

Below. Detail of the guipure lace-over-satin dress, made by an unknown dressmaker, that Grace Kelly wore to receive her Philadelphia Arts Award.

subdued clothes, considered completely American, were widely available, and retailers were alerted to the fresh promotional direction offered by the 'Grace Kelly Look'.[31]

By late December 1955, when the Associated Press named Grace Kelly woman of the year in entertainment, they applauded the actress's professional achievements but emphasized her fashion influence. The actress, they asserted, had inspired both new standards of film beauty and the fresh, young 'American Look' seen in current collections — 'Grace Kelly, a nice girl from a nice family, has made good taste glamorous'.[32] On 5 January 1956 it was announced that she had earned a place on the Best-Dressed List for the second time. She had been ranked at the bottom the previous year, but, in 'an almost unprecedented rise', she topped the list of 1955, tied for first place with the perennial favourite Barbara 'Babe' Cushing Mortimer Paley.[33] Babe Paley, a former fashion editor who had married first a member of the Standard Oil family and then the head of CBS, was said to buy most

of her wardrobe from Mainbocher, one of the world's most expensive couturiers. Grace Kelly's clothes-buying habits provided an obvious contrast, and her age and social role were also very different; both women, however, were tall and slender and were said to 'prefer simple clothes'. By selecting these two women as current fashion leaders, the American fashion press was said to have implicitly endorsed sophisticated simplicity and 'well-bred elegance rather than startling effect as its own ideal'.[34]

On the same day that the Best-Dressed List of 1955 was released, Grace Kelly made news in another way by announcing her engagement to Prince Rainier III of Monaco. In a few short years she had risen to the top of the acting profession and had become a respected leader of fashion. The elegant, understated style that she had made famous would henceforth be worn by a celebrated bride and princess-to-be.

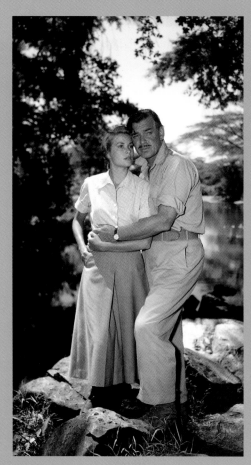

HELEN ROSE

The costume designer Helen Rose (1904–1985) spent her career working for the film studio Metro-Goldwyn-Mayer (MGM), designing costumes for more than 200 films, receiving two Academy Awards and a further eight nominations. MGM was known for their sparkling costume designs and Rose furthered this reputation, creating elegant yet fashionable costumes for the studio's actors and actresses. Rose was originally from Chicago, and her background was in fine art. She studied at the art academy in Chicago and then worked at Lester Costume Company and Ernie Young's costume house, where she costumed vaudeville and nightclub performers. She gained crucial experience working on these theatrical productions, particularly working with fabrics such as chiffon and synthetics, which would prove useful during her costume design career. Rose moved to Hollywood in 1929 to work for a wardrobe company that supplied various film studios. This led to a job designing for the 'Ice Follies', a popular and elaborate touring show on ice.

In 1943 MGM offered Rose a position designing at the studio, which was still in transition after the retirement of the illustrious Adrian, who had designed for the studio's films throughout the 1930s and '40s, including *The Wizard of Oz* (1939). In her first few years there, she concentrated on designing clothes for the younger stars of the studio, but worked her way up to chief costume designer. She costumed leading ladies Ava Gardner, Cyd Charisse, Jane Powell, Lena Horne, Grace Kelly, Elizabeth Taylor, Ann Blyth, Debbie Reynolds and Pier Angeli, among many others, also designing wedding dresses, day wear and glamorous evening wear for the stars to wear off screen. Her style favoured a strong silhouette, with carefully chosen decoration striking a balance between theatricality and functionality. Rose produced clothes that were similar in quality to high-end ready-to-wear, clothing to which film audiences could aspire.

Rose was known for designing costumes that had mass appeal with both the public and manufacturers. Dresses created for films including *Father of the Bride* (1950) were extensively copied by designers on both coasts of the United States, as was the white gathered chiffon dress worn by Liz Taylor in *Cat on a Hot Tin Roof* (1958), with Taylor asking for a copy of the dress to be made for her personal wardrobe. With Rose's designs in demand, she entered into the wholesale garment business, selling expensive ready-to-wear to exclusive department stores and boutiques throughout the United States, eventually leaving MGM in 1966. She also pursued writing, with a regular fashion column, and completed her autobiography, *Just Make Them Beautiful*, in 1976. s.e.s

---

Helen Rose and Grace Kelly worked together on several MGM films including *Mogambo*, filmed in Kenya in 1953 (top left), and *The Swan*, filmed in 1955. This publicity shot from the latter, set in the early twentieth century, was much reprinted when it was announced that Helen Rose would design the actress's real-life wedding dress for her marriage to Prince Rainier (bottom). Another wedding dress was required for Grace Kelly's final film, *High Society* (1956), when her character remarries her ex-husband, played by Bing Crosby (top right).

OLEG CASSINI

Oleg Cassini (1913–2006) is best known for creating the wardrobe of First Lady Jacqueline Kennedy in the 1960s, a look based on American principles of sportswear integrated with elements from European couturiers. He was born in Paris to aristocratic Russian parents, and the family moved around Europe before settling in Florence, Italy. Here, Cassini was exposed to the fashion business by his mother, who opened a couture house on Via Tornabuoni. He attended university and art school in Florence before moving to Paris to pursue a career in fashion design.

Cassini's design career, spanning 70 years, included employment at Patou in Paris as a sketch artist, a short-lived venture in Rome, and producing couture and ready-to-wear clothes for several companies under his own name in New York. He moved to Hollywood in 1940, where Paramount Pictures hired him as the design assistant to Edith Head. He met and married the actress Gene Tierney whilst working for Paramount, and designed costumes for her film *The Razor's Edge* (1946). Upon leaving this position, Cassini entered into another short-lived business called Casanova, selling off-the-peg gabardine suits. This business too collapsed, but in 1950 Cassini secured substantial funding to establish his ready-to-wear company in New York. This company was successful, producing overtly feminine and romantic gowns using taffetas, embroidery, lace and chiffon, but also sharply tailored suits with military details such as buttons, braids and pockets. In 1954 Cassini met Grace Kelly and she wore several of his designs.

In 1961 Cassini became the official designer for Jacqueline Kennedy, and worked with the First Lady to create her public wardrobe, consisting of gently fitted evening and cocktail dresses cut in straight lines, boxy jacket and skirt suits with covered buttons, sleeveless jersey shell blouses and A-line skirts and dresses. For John F. Kennedy's swearing-in ceremony, Kennedy wore a Cassini-designed beige wool crêpe dress accessorized with her trademark pillbox hat, bringing his designs to worldwide attention. His successful designs for Kennedy and his elite clientele enabled the company to expand into swimwear, handbags, hosiery, gloves, menswear and costume jewellery. By the end of the 1960s Cassini had disbanded his high-end ready-to-wear lines, but his licensing business remained successful throughout the 1970s. Cassini's autobiography, *In My Own Fashion*, was published in 1987. s.e.s

Cassini, who met Grace Kelly in 1954, was her on-and-off beau before her engagement. The actress wore several of his designs, including this dramatic evening dress; she is shown with the designer at the charity premiere of the film *Desirée* on 17 November 1954.

EDITH HEAD

The costume designer Edith Head (1897–1981) clothed Hollywood's most illustrious film stars during her 58-year career. Noted for her skill in defining character through the use of costume, Head won the Academy Award eight times, and received a total of 35 nominations in her lifetime. She originally trained as a teacher, specializing in languages, and during her first career took evening classes to perfect her drawing. In 1923 she answered an advertisement for a sketch artist position at Famous Players-Lasky (later Paramount studios). The chief costume designer, Howard Greer (who had been an apprentice to the famous British designer Lucile, Lady Duff Gordon), was taken with her work and Head was hired. Four years later Greer left Paramount and Head was promoted to assistant designer under Travis Banton. In this role, she was able to hone her costuming skills on B-movie stars and extras, working towards a restrained and dignified aesthetic that ultimately led to her promotion as chief designer for Paramount in 1938, where she worked until 1967. She then became chief designer at Universal Studios until her death in 1981.

Head was known for her 'character' costumes for actors such as Olivia de Havilland in *The Heiress* (1949), which secured her first Oscar, and Gloria Swanson in *Sunset Boulevard* (1950). Her collaborations with Alfred Hitchcock were also highly effective, since the director was convinced of the importance of dress in film. As chief designer on *Rear Window* (1954), Head was introduced to its star, Grace Kelly, and a long-lasting friendship and working relationship was established. Besides Grace Kelly, she designed for Elizabeth Taylor, Audrey Hepburn, Ginger Rogers, Bette Davis, Shirley MacLaine, Joanne Woodward and Kim Novak, among many others.

Known for her ability to please difficult film stars and to correct imperfect figures with her sensitive designs, Head had a wider influence on fashion, enhanced by a recurring role dispensing fashion advice on Art Linkletter's radio and television programme *House Party*. She also wrote two fashion advice books, *The Dress Doctor* (1959) and *How to Dress for Success* (1967), as well as an autobiography, *Edith Head's Hollywood* (1983). Head's trademark dark glasses (originally worn to assess designs in black-and-white film) and her unchanging hairstyle of a short flat fringe pulled into a sharp chignon at the back marked her out from colleagues within the industry. Her classic, pared-down approach to design stamped her work with a lasting elegance. *S.E.S*

Edith Head (top left) and Grace Kelly established a lasting and friendly working relationship on the set of *Rear Window* (1954). Grace Kelly's impressive costumes were an obvious contrast to the pyjamas worn by co-star James Stewart throughout the film and were vital to the plot and the development of her character (top right and bottom right). Head's costumes for *To Catch a Thief* (1954), with its glamorous setting in the south of France, included alluring beachwear (bottom left).

Grace Kelly Style

THE BRIDE

In May 1955 Grace Kelly attended the Cannes Film Festival in the south of France. She had been to the festival the previous year and had also filmed *To Catch a Thief* in the area, but this visit was to change the course of her life. The young actress — a successful, independent career woman acknowledged as the 'Queen of Hollywood' — felt that her fame was empty without someone to share it, and her meeting with Prince Rainier III, ruler of the small principality of Monaco, came at the perfect time for both. Their 'fairy-tale' betrothal and the royal wedding ceremonies that followed captured public imagination and brought new attention to the bride's tasteful style.

s part of the publicity that went along with the Cannes Film Festival, the French magazine *Paris Match* arranged for a photo shoot in nearby Monaco to feature Grace Kelly and Prince Rainier. The actress's busy schedule allowed little time for the excursion, and the appointed day did not begin auspiciously. A power cut at her hotel meant that the harried star could not dry and style her hair, so with an assistant she improvised a pulled-back coiffure decorated with a small floral headpiece. Unable to iron a dress, she donned her only unwrinkled outfit, a floral silk taffeta dress quite different from the sleek, understated ensembles she usually selected. The shiny, crisp fabric was warp-printed with a bold floral pattern, and the cut was fussy — it had a squared neckline and long tight sleeves, and was described as 'long-waisted, with a wide hip sash' above the full skirt. Although it was later said to be 'Dior-inspired' and 'with a definite couture look', the dress was not a designer creation but an 'easy to sew' dress from McCall Patterns made of 5 yards of 35-inch-wide material;[1] the actress had worn

Left. In May 1955 Grace Kelly attended the Cannes Film Festival, not far from Monaco. A photo shoot in the principality, arranged by the magazine *Paris Match*, brought about her momentous meeting with Prince Rainier.

Right. The illustration on McCall's pattern for the dress Grace Kelly wore to meet Prince Rainier. The actress had modelled the dress on the cover of their spring pattern book of 1955.

it — with white gloves and a close-fitting asymmetrical floral headpiece — on the
cover of McCall's pattern book of spring 1955.

Grace Kelly's small party arrived at the Monégasque palace on time, despite
a minor accident, but she found that the prince was delayed and had to pose alone
in various locations. When Prince Rainier finally arrived they toured the state
apartments, the museum and the prince's private zoo. Although at the time she was
romantically linked to the dashing French actor Jean-Pierre Aumont, Grace Kelly
found the prince 'charming'. The brief meeting made a deep impression on both of
them; although they did not meet again until the end of the year, by the New Year
they had decided to get married.

Grace Kelly and Prince Rainier announced their engagement on 5 January 1956.
Announcements were made both in Monaco and by the couple themselves during
a small luncheon at the Philadelphia Country Club. A single photographer was
permitted there, but by the time the couple arrived at the Kelly family home in
East Falls news of the betrothal had spread via international bulletins. More than a
hundred media representatives swarmed over the house and photographed the
prince and princess-to-be as they arrived, capturing the chic star wearing sunglasses,
a fur coat and white gloves, and carrying a Hermès *haut à courroies* handbag — the
bag that would later be dubbed the 'Kelly' bag.[2]

For the betrothal announcement, Grace Kelly had chosen a favourite dress from
her wardrobe in one of the styles most associated with her tasteful look, a classic
shirtwaist dress. The champagne-coloured silk dress with gold brocade dots was
made by the New York fashion house of Branell for their moderately priced ready-

to-wear resort collection of 1955. Described as combining rich fabric with great simplicity, it featured a box-pleated skirt, three-quarter-length sleeves with cuffs and a small, shaped shawl collar.[3] A gold brooch was pinned to the collar, which matched the actress's gold earrings, and she filled in the neckline with a beige chiffon scarf. For two hours the couple answered reporters' questions and obligingly posed for photographs, although they refused to kiss. The future princess showed off her engagement ring of entwined rubies and diamonds, stones that echoed the national colours of Monaco; her fiancé would soon supplement this with a 12-carat diamond ring.

Grace Kelly's forthcoming marriage came as a complete surprise to her friends and fans. Newspapers across the United States and Europe splashed the story across their front pages. Hollywood was flabbergasted by the news that 'Screen Queen' Grace Kelly was to marry Prince Rainier Louis Henri Maxence Bertrand Grimaldi, the sovereign of the smallest secular state in the world.

While Prince Rainier was relatively unknown to the American public, *Life* magazine noted that he was one of the world's most eligible bachelors.[4] Born in 1923, the Catholic prince had been educated in Britain and France and had served with the Forces Françaises Libres (Free French Forces) during the Second World War. In 1949 his mother's father had abdicated in his favour, making him the reigning Prince of Monaco. The Grimaldi were Europe's oldest ruling family: except for two short breaks, they had ruled Monaco since 1297, when François Grimaldi had captured the Genoese fortress from rivals by disguising himself as a friar. For centuries, however, Spain, France and the Italian states sought control over Monaco. In 1861 the Franco-Monégasque Treaty finally recognized Monaco's sovereignty, and in the late nineteenth century the opening of the Monte Carlo Casino and the abolishment of all taxes attracted both visitors and residents. By 1956 Monaco had some 20,000 residents, of whom 2,500 were Monégasque subjects, and tourism was one of the country's principal sources of income. A treaty of 1918 that provided limited French protection over Monaco also stipulated that if the reigning prince failed to provide an heir to the throne, Monaco would revert to France.

Prince Rainier and Grace Kelly made their first public appearance together the night after their engagement announcement, attending a large charity ball at the

Left. On 6 January 1956 Prince Rainier and Grace Kelly attended a large charity ball at the Waldorf-Astoria in New York. The bride-to-be wore a strapless white gown by Christian Dior–New York, adding a red and white orchid corsage in tribute to Monaco.

Above. After completing the filming of *High Society*, Grace Kelly stayed in California so that she could attend the Academy Awards, since it was traditional for the previous year's winner of the best actress award to present the award for best actor. She attended the ceremony on 22 March 1956 wearing a dress designed by Helen Rose.

Waldorf-Astoria in New York. The future princess was the centre of attention in a strapless white ball gown by Christian Dior–New York, which she accented with a red and white orchid corsage in tribute to Monaco. The following day she returned to California to start filming *High Society*, but interest in the star, her prince, their 'fairy-tale' romance and the royal wedding continued. During the following months almost-daily bulletins recounted every detail for a fascinated public: in early April *Women's Wear Daily* asserted that 'in recent weeks, almost no newspaper went to press without at least one mention of Grace Kelly'.[5]

With her engagement to Prince Rainier, the already sizable influence that Grace Kelly had on fashion intensified. She continued to be placed on best-dressed lists for her tasteful style of dressing, the 'Grace Kelly Look' that she had inspired in late 1955 became big fashion news for spring 1956, and the star was credited with putting 'her stamp on the fashions of the season, starting to influence trends as few women have'.[6] The style set by the actress and famous fiancée now spread beyond the United States, influencing all things fashionable in France. Thanks to Grace Kelly, casual clothes on the Riviera were said to be tailored with American dash and beach fashions were less revealing.[7] In Paris, the fashion press noted, haute couture collections reflected the actress's tasteful style — 'ladylike, genteel, and most serene'.[8] Designers favoured the type of clothes that best suited the star, along with discreet necklines and hemlines, 'bridal white' and colours flattering to the fair-haired.[9] Both French and American models also adopted the 'Grace Kelly Look': wholesome, dignified, ladylike models were in high demand, and their hair — blond by nature or design — was often styled *à la Grace*.[10]

Given Grace Kelly's status as a fashion icon, there was naturally special interest in her trousseau and her bridal clothes — she would need ensembles for both the cathedral wedding and the civil marriage ceremony required by Monégasque law. Both bridal ensembles, it was announced on 23 January, would be presents to the star from MGM; their chief costume designer, Helen Rose, got the much-coveted honour of designing the wedding gowns, which would be specially created by the skilled workers in the studio's wardrobe department.

Although the filming of *High Society* in Hollywood had finished by mid-March, Grace Kelly postponed her departure for New York by a week in order to present the Academy Award for best actor. She had found little time to purchase her trousseau and felt that her wedding preparations were behind schedule, but nevertheless left California with the beginnings of her bridal wardrobe. MGM gave its star a dozen Helen Rose-designed outfits from *High Society*; since these were created for the film's summer resort setting, the designer pointed out that they would be perfect for wear on the Riviera. Helen Rose had also thrown Grace Kelly a bridal shower in California, and several more showers were held for her in New York and Philadelphia.

Once back on the East Coast, wedding preparations kept Grace Kelly very busy indeed. Her friend, the fashion expert Eleanor Lambert, used her insider knowledge and industry connections to enable the bride-to-be to make the most of her limited time in New York and to preview designers' as yet unreleased summer collections. The star's trousseau shopping was rapid and intense — and fascinating to others. Enormous crowds gathered wherever she went, forcing her to shop early in the morning, and photographers and reporters trailed after her, recording her every action 'for an insatiably inquisitive world'.[11]

When the whirl of shopping was done, her trousseau contained some 40 outfits, including day clothes, cocktail dresses, short and long evening dresses, suits and coats, and featured both full-skirted and slim silhouettes. The colour palette included beige in shades of almost white to amber, delicate pastels that suited the actress's blond hair and fair complexion, blue in shades from turquoise to sapphire to navy, and her favourite colour, yellow.[12] Discussions of the trousseau noted the absence of black, which Monaco's reigning family wore for evening only while in mourning, and some predicted the colour might consequently suffer a major fashion eclipse.[13]

The future bride's patronage was widespread. She ordered garments and accessories through Los Angeles retailers, Philadelphia shops and New York department stores and specialty shops. As one fashion editor declared, the names represented in the trousseau made up almost a 'who's who' of American designers.[14] They included James Galanos, Harvey Berin, Fira Benenson, Pauline Trigère, Ceil Chapman, Traina-

Grace Kelly, with her mother and sister, arriving at a bridal shower in New York. The future bride wears a fur coat and a pink toque decorated with silk roses.

For her trousseau, Grace Kelly chose garments from 40 of America's top designers, and ordered from shops in Los Angeles, New York and Philadelphia. As this article from the *Philadelphia Inquirer* of 17 April 1956 shows, her all-American wardrobe was hailed as both supremely tasteful and a significant promotion of American design.

The True Story Is Told

Grace's Luxurious Trousseau Shows Good Taste

40 Costumes By Top U. S. Designers

By CYNTHIA CABOT
Fashion Editor

Norell, Samuel Winston, Adele Simpson, Mollie Parnis, Larry Aldrich, Christian Dior–New York, Branell, Ben Zuckerman, Suzy Perette, Marquise and B.H. Wragge.[15]

While she ordered four furs from Leo Ritter, the pragmatic bride also bought plenty of sports clothes, including a Claire McCardell bathing suit, and made sure she had 'oodles of shorts, slacks, and sun dresses for lounging on the yachting honeymoon'.[16] Although much of the trousseau was in silk, Grace Kelly selected three full-skirted, thin cotton dresses from John Carter of Beverly Hills.[17] Nor did she neglect accessories, a major part of her ladylike look; these all complemented her usual beige and blue ensembles, and included silk chiffon scarves, almost 30 pairs of shoes and many hats — ranging from small satin chignons to large toques — from a number of leading American milliners.[18]

Merchants and designers were delighted to supply the celebrated and stylish bride. 'Of course, it's easy to dress her', one designer told a reporter. 'She has the ideal body to build a dress on — you just can't go wrong.'[19] To show their appreciation, many presented items that she had ordered as gifts. Seventh Avenue staffs worked overtime to finish her garments; Ben Zuckerman, one of her favourite designers, was reportedly so rushed filling her order that he had to delay work on his autumn and winter collection.

Grace Kelly's trousseau purchases were seen by the fashion press as a powerful stimulant to the garment trade, since the many women avidly following her much-publicized shopping sprees would naturally be inspired to add to their own wardrobes. That she bought an all-American wardrobe was also considered a significant promotion of American design: the star would wear her new clothes in her future life as a princess, and show the world that she 'comes from a country with dress designers of great distinction, equal to any in the world'.[20]

On 4 April 1956 Grace Kelly boarded the SS *Constitution* at New York's Pier 84 for the voyage to Monaco. She did not set sail alone: she was 'accompanied by an entourage of 80 and with 60 pieces of luggage and a trousseau befitting a princess'.[21] Before the ship sailed, several hundred members of the press attended a press conference on the sun deck; although this threatened to become a riot, the future princess appeared 'cool as a cucumber' in a beige suit as she answered questions and waved her white-gloved hand.[22]

While the bride spent the eight days of the trip relaxing and enjoying the company of her family and friends, everything she did and everything she wore attracted attention. On board, one report stated: 'All the passengers are waiting to see what Grace will wear.'[23] Those on land were informed that, while her day clothes leaned toward casual skirts and practical headscarves, for evening she wore some new garments from her trousseau, including an evening gown she had worn in *High Society*, as well as old favourites from her wardrobe. One of the latter was from the autumn 1954 collection of Oleg Cassini, her former beau. Made of white lace, the dress had a full skirt, bracelet-length sleeves and neckline that was high across the front but dipped in a wide V at the back to a velvet bow at the waistline. As the

On 4 April 1956 Grace Kelly held an impromptu press conference, facing a mass of journalists and photographers on the SS *Constitution* before sailing for Monaco. Her beige tailored suit was worn with immaculate white accessories.

During the eight days and nights of the voyage, the future princess and her clothes remained the focus of press attention. For evening wear she wore some of her new trousseau gowns, but was also photographed playing a game of charades in an old favourite, a lace dress by Oleg Cassini.

finale of the designer's fashion show in New York of July 1954, the lace dress had been called 'the absolute end in elegance'.[24] Photographers had captured the star wearing the dress in New York in late 1954 and during the Cannes Film Festival of 1955. Numerous shipboard photographs by Howell Conant, published in a photo spread in *Life*, show the future princess wearing the becoming lace dress once more to play charades; despite employing all her dramatic talents during the intense game, both she and the dress retained their elegance.[25]

On 12 April the SS *Constitution* arrived in Monaco, where as many as 50,000 spectators — twice the principality's population — had assembled to welcome the future princess. Although only 500 could attend the cathedral wedding, and the civil ceremony was even more exclusive, the tiny principality of Monaco was overwhelmed with wedding guests. Some were lucky enough to be invited to other wedding-week festivities, which included a full schedule of receptions, galas, dinners, ballets, athletic events, fireworks and other celebratory fêtes.

The press was also there in force — 1,800 had been accredited to cover the wedding; they competed for access and newsworthy tidbits, and, when these were not forthcoming, created stories out of almost anything.

Once outside the harbour at Monaco, Grace Kelly boarded a tender to meet her fiancé on his yacht. She then disembarked in the picturesque harbour, and was warmly welcomed by officials, an honour guard, salutes, flowers and an ovation from the crowd. For the occasion, she chose an off-the-peg but modish ensemble she had just purchased from Ben Zuckerman, a Romanian-born émigré who, starting as an errand boy in New York's garment district, had become an acknowledged master tailor. His sleeveless silk alpaca sheath and matching coat were in navy, the colour of the season. The coat featured a small collar, three-quarter-length sleeves and a self-tie at the high waist above pleats. The bride-to-be wore a bunch of imitation white violets on the front, exactly as shown in an advertisement for the coat in

Grace Kelly, escorted by her future husband, disembarked in the harbour at Monaco, and was welcomed by officials and crowds of spectators. She wore a matching navy blue silk dress and coat by Ben Zuckerman of New York with a fashionable but troublesome wide-brimmed hat.

February's *Harper's Bazaar*, but personalized her outfit with pearl earrings and bracelet, a white scarf crossed inside her V neckline and short white gloves. One accessory she chose — a white organdie hat — attracted the most attention, as well as a fair amount of criticism; although the broad, mushroom-shaped brim was the height of current fashion, it had to be held in the breeze and, most egregiously, hid her famously beautiful face from her future subjects and eager photographers. Soon after her arrival, a closed car whisked

the bride off to the palace, where she made a brief appearance to wave from the balcony before retiring.

The following day the prince drove his fiancée — wearing the tiniest of hats — to luncheon with his sister.[26] Over-eager photographers mobbed the couple's car, and the prince reacted by barring the media from palace events. As the wedding week continued, the press became increasingly desperate for information and images, and even booed the couple after one gala when they failed to stop in the rain to be photographed. Cordial relations were restored by the wedding rehearsal in the cathedral on 16 April, however, when 50 photographers were allowed to record the event. The next day also provided plenty of news fodder: MGM finally released the long-awaited descriptions and sketches of both the formal religious gown and the civil wedding suit, and the betrothed couple officially received wedding presents, which included an open-top cream and black Rolls-Royce from the Monégasque people. For this ceremony in the palace courtyard, the bride selected from her trousseau a delicate pale blue chiffon day dress by the California designer James Galanos.[27] The dress's face-framing, large, round collar and ribbon bow emphasized Grace Kelly's youth and beauty; while her hat of matching ribbon was suitably miniscule, she made news by wearing high heels that accentuated her height.

The civil marriage of Grace Kelly and Prince Rainier took place in the palace throne room on the morning of 18 April. The 40-minute ceremony was performed in front of approximately 80 guests by Monaco's highest legal authority, the minister of justice. Both the groom, in formal morning dress, and the bride seemed strained, no doubt affected by the solemnity of the occasion.

The bride was, however, beautiful in the beige lace and dusty rose silk suit that Helen Rose had designed. According to an announcement made by MGM the previous day, Grace Kelly's civil ceremony outfit, while 'naturally not so elaborate as the formal gown', was 'designed with equal care'.[28] The fitted bodice had a rounded

collar and silk-cord bow at the high neck and closed down the front with lace-covered buttons; the skirt flared into a full hem at 14 inches above the floor. The fabric, detailed by MGM's embroiderers to produce an unusual effect, added interest to the simple suit: over a foundation of what MGM called 'ashes of roses taffeta', the floral pattern of the machine-made 'blush-tan' lace was outlined with dusty pink silk floss embroidery for additional depth.[29] The accessories that completed the bridal ensemble were also carefully considered and constructed. A small, close-fitting hat trimmed with silk flowers, designed by Helen Rose, sat prettily on the back of the head. Dusty pink silk pumps with lace overlay to match the suit were created by leading American shoe designer David Evins. Short white gloves added the final touch.

After taking their vows, the couple was pronounced legally married. The prince and his bride, now Her Serene Highness Grace Patricia of Monaco, relaxed and joined 2,500 joyful Monégasque subjects in the palace garden. The celebrations continued that night at an elaborate gala at the opera. The new princess was radiant, wearing a diamond tiara and necklace given to her by the people of Monaco and dressed in an embroidered ivory gown specially designed by Antonio Castillo of the Paris fashion house Lanvin-Castillo to show off the decorations and orders that her husband had bestowed (see p.64).

On the morning of 19 April, the cathedral of Saint Nicholas was filled with guests and its exterior was enlivened by a red carpet, white silk wedding canopy and uniformed cordon of honour. The bride and her father arrived in a black Rolls-Royce, ascended the steps and proceeded down the aisle. Princess Grace took her place at the prie-dieu. Her two ring bearers entered, followed by four flower girls, her oldest sister as matron of honour and her six bridesmaids in pairs. The royal groom came down the aisle a few moments later wearing a wedding outfit that he had designed himself. Based on the uniform of Napoleon's marshals, it included a black tunic with gold-embroidered cuffs and epaulettes and sky-blue trousers with a gold stripe down the sides, and was embellished with medals, orders, aiguillettes, the sash of the Order of St Charles and a sword.

His bride, however, was more than a match for this princely plumage, thanks to her natural beauty and her simple yet magnificent wedding dress. Helen Rose had designed the gown to set off but not overpower the bride. The bodice was made of a type of antique lace known in the United States and described by MGM as 'rose point' lace; it had a high neck, tiny buttons down the centre front and long sleeves over a strapless underbodice. The floral and scroll motifs of the lace had been reassembled and re-embroidered so that the bodice appeared seamless, and tiny seed pearls and three-dimensional petals accented the lace pattern. A high cummerbund of ivory silk faille encircled the bride's slim waist, now measuring less than 21 inches due to the strain of the past few months. The full silk faille skirt was bell-shaped, with heavy pleats at the waist across the sides and at the back, and three petticoats and a short hoop skirt for support. The back of the skirt had three bows and a triangular inset of lace that flowed into the graceful train. The bridal headpiece, made from pearl-embellished lace motifs, was decorated with a crown-like wreath of delicate wax orange blossoms, tiny floral lace motifs stiffened with wire, and leaves fashioned from seed pearls. The silk tulle oval veil, specially designed to keep the bride's face on view, was edged with rose point lace motifs accented with seed pearls, and had two small lace lovebirds appliquéd at the back. The shoes, custom-made by David Evins, continued the pearl and lace theme. Even the tiny bride's prayer manual that Grace Kelly elected to carry had been decorated with matching lace and seed pearls.[30] According to MGM, creating Grace Kelly's cathedral bridal ensemble had taken six weeks and involved the skills of 35 studio craftspeople, working under strict conditions to preserve the secrecy of the design.

The happy couple shortly after the ceremony in Monaco's cathedral of Saint Nicholas. Prince Rainier wore a uniform he had designed himself to set off his medals and orders. His bride's gown was simple but magnificent, with a lace cap, veil and bodice, and a cummerbund and full trained skirt of silk faille.

Inside the cathedral, the Bishop of Monaco and the bride's parish priest spoke, and then the bishop conducted the solemn marriage ceremony. After the exchange of vows and rings, the couple was pronounced joined in holy matrimony. Mass was celebrated, and a papal emissary offered the pope's blessing and delivered an address. The prince and princess then proceeded slowly down the aisle and down the steps.

Outside the cathedral, trumpets sounded and the newly-weds took their places in their new open-top Rolls-Royce. The motorcade drove slowly through the streets of Monaco as thousands waved joyfully and church bells pealed. Following a Monégasque wedding tradition, the procession stopped at the tiny church of Sainte Devote for the bride to leave her small bouquet of lilies of the valley as an offering to the patron saint of Monaco.

The royal couple returned to the palace, where they posed for more photographs and waved from a window to the crowd waiting outside. In the palace courtyard, they joined their guests for an elegant buffet luncheon and cut the five-tiered wedding cake. The prince and princess soon slipped away to change clothes for their honeymoon departure. Princess Grace, in a light grey silk suit designed by her friend Edith Head,[31] and the prince, wearing a dark double-breasted jacket, made their way through the waving and cheering crowds to the harbour, and shortly after five o'clock departed for a restful and private month-long honeymoon aboard the royal yacht.

During her months as a renowned bride-to-be, Grace Kelly's classic style had exerted great fashion influence; as a film star turned royal bride, her appearance during the famous wedding — seen by millions on television and in print coverage — set the standard for understated elegance. She now began her new life as Princess of Monaco.

Right. Following their wedding reception, Prince Rainier and Princess Grace board the royal yacht *Deo Juvente II* for their relaxing honeymoon. The princess wears a light grey silk suit designed by Edith Head.

LANVIN

Lanvin is the oldest surviving couture house in continuous existence. Records show that Jeanne Lanvin (1867–1946) was a millinery apprentice working for Madame Felix trimming hats on rue du Faubourg Saint-Honoré in 1883, and she opened her own millinery workshop two years later at the age of 18. By 1889 Lanvin had opened a millinery house in an apartment at 16, rue Boissy-d'Anglais, and a children's clothing department was established within the millinery shop in 1908.

Lanvin was inspired by the clothes she designed for her only daughter, Marguerite Marie-Blanche, and she became well known for her matching mother-and-daughter outfits. Her designs were characterized by long, lean, empire-waist silhouettes and styles that afforded movement, especially the full skirt of 1915–16 that she recreated throughout the years with only slight adjustments. Her creations often featured dazzling beading and embroidery patterns. By 1925 she was employing 800 people, and her label had expanded to include 23 ateliers, with branches in Cannes and Le Touquet, as well as international shops in Buenos Aires and Barcelona. Lanvin launched departments for menswear, furs, lingerie and several successful fragrance lines. Jeanne Lanvin died in 1946 and her daughter Marie-Blanche became the chairman and managing director of the house and of Lanvin perfumes until her death in 1958. The designing of this unequivocally French label changed hands frequently. In 1950 it became Lanvin-Castillo, when Antonio Canovas del Castillo became creative director. He reinvigorated the label, whilst retaining a great respect for the traditions of the company. The Madrid-born Castillo brought a distinctive new emphasis on brighter colours, contrasting combinations of light and heavy textiles, and a more restrained form of sophistication to the house style. He had previously worked with Piguet and Paquin in Paris, and spent five years in New York working for Elizabeth Arden.

In 1963 Castillo left to set up his own couture house, and the label reverted back to Lanvin. The French investor group Harmonie S.A. bought the house in 2001, and in the following year Alber Elbaz began designing the high-end women's wear collections, once again reviving the label, which is now recognized as one of the most desirable luxury fashion brands. *S.E.S*

Princess Grace selected several outfits from the Lanvin-Castillo collections, perhaps partly because the fashion house was owned by a branch of the Polignac family, relations of Prince Rainier. Made for her trousseau, this spectacular example was worn by the princess to several formal occasions, and she is photographed here with Prince Rainier by Howell Conant soon after her marriage. The dress was specially designed for the princess to wear with the sash, star and badge of the Monégasque Order of St Charles.

CHRISTIAN DIOR

Christian Dior (1905–1957) was one of the most famous couturiers of the twentieth century, and dominated fashion in the late 1940s and '50s with his elegant and sumptuous designs. As a student in Paris, Dior befriended many avant-garde artists, and in 1927, after military service, he opened an art gallery, exhibiting such artists as Dalí and Picasso. At the age of 30, Dior turned to studying, drawing and designing fashion, and in 1936 he became a fashion illustrator at *Le Figaro*. The following year Robert Piguet offered him a position in his couture studio. Dior was mobilized during the war, and afterwards worked for the respected couturier Lucien Lelong.

On 8 October 1946 Dior opened his own couture house in a private mansion on 30, avenue Montaigne, with financial backing from textile manufacturer Marcel Boussac. The house had four models, 85 employees and two workshops, one for dresses and one for tailoring, the latter directed by the young Pierre Cardin. Dior's 'Corolle' collection, which became known as the 'New Look', debuted in 1947, sending shock waves through the fashion world. It has been said that this collection brought back the vogue for overt femininity with corseted waists and wide skirts made from up to 50 yards of material.

Dior's designs sculpted the body into a pleasing silhouette. Nipped-in waists and swelling hips — or the reverse — all featured prominently. He favoured sumptuous fabrics, from thick taffetas, satins and velvets to fine shantung and the softest chiffon. Surfaces were heavily embellished with embroidery, artificial flowers, beading, or lace, taking inspiration from Belle Epoque fashions. Wealthy and glamorous women across the world wanted to wear Dior designs, and the designer responded to demand, opening the subsidiary Christian Dior–New York in 1948, and establishing other Dior companies in London, Australia and South America. The Dior empire eventually included separate divisions retailing accessories, gifts and tableware.

Dior died from a heart attack in 1957 at the age of 52. Worldwide pressure prevented Marcel Boussac from closing the house, and the youthful Yves Saint Laurent, Dior's design assistant from 1955, was named as artistic director. Saint Laurent moved away from Dior's sophisticated aesthetic, with radical designs such as the 'Beat Look'. He was called up for service in 1960 to fight in the Algerian War of Independence, and in 1961 Marc Bohan became Dior's artistic director. Gianfranco Ferre took over from Bohan in 1989; since 1997 John Galliano has injected spectacle and fantasy into the brand, leading it into the twenty-first century. *S.E.S*

Before her marriage, Grace Kelly was a loyal customer of the Christian Dior–New York label. Here, she is pictured with Alfred Hitchcock and James Stewart wearing a Christian Dior–New York gown to the premiere of *Rear Window* on 14 August 1954 (bottom). Two years later, on 6 January 1956, the night after her engagement was announced, she wore a white strapless silk gown at a charity gala at the Waldorf-Astoria, New York (top right). As a princess, she wore the label's grey lightweight wool suit for travelling, seen here at the Gare de Lyon in Paris on 4 September 1956 (top left).

MAGGY ROUFF

Maggy Rouff (1876–1971) began her dress-making career at Drecoll in Paris, where her mother was head of design and her father the business manager. She designed for Drecoll until 1929, when she opened her own couture house. She owed her initial success and the establishment of her reputation to the public's fascination with the silver screen — her gowns were worn by icons of the early cinema such as Theda Bara, Pola Negri and Greta Garbo. The suits and day dresses she designed often incorporated scarves that could be tied into various forms such as a collar or bow, and were enhanced by belts, wide sashes, buttons and details that were decorative but also functional. Evening wear was often characterized by harmonious draping, with soft cowl necks, ruching or sarong-like skirt panels with enriched surfaces that featured quilting, appliqué or fur, a mainstay within her collections.

In 1937, as the house grew, Maggy Rouff opened a salon in London, where her Parisian gowns were shown to her large British clientele. The next year she published the first of three books, *Ce que j'ai vu en chiffonnant la clientèle*, which was followed in 1942 by *La Philosophie de l'élégance*, written while Paris was occupied by German troops during the Second World War. After Rouff's retirement from the label in 1948, her daughter, Anne-Marie Besançon de Wagner, began designing for the house, keeping to Rouff's strict attitude towards dress. During the 1950s Maggy Rouff evening designs reflected the trend for full skirts and floor-length gowns with trains, while her chic daywear featured fur-trimmed swing coats and belted wool dresses.

Besançon de Wagner retired in the early 1960s, when the house switched its focus from couture to ready-to-wear, with three different designers working on the collection for a few seasons. The line ultimately failed to keep up with the more radical designs being produced by younger couturiers and boutique owners in London and in Paris. The date the company closed is unknown, although Claire Barrat, a former apprentice, attempted to revive the label in 1976. *S.E.S*

In a photograph taken by Howell Conant at the Princely Palace of Monaco soon after the marriage, Princess Grace wore a fairy-tale Rouff gown of shell pink with a swathe of sequin-studded net around the shoulders and a waist-cinching belt. She also wore this gown, a grey wool maternity dress and at least one other Rouff evening gown on a trip to the US in late 1958.

HUBERT DE GIVENCHY

Hubert de Givenchy (b.1927) is best known for his grand evening wear, functional yet elegant daywear and his design collaboration with the actress Audrey Hepburn. In 1944 Givenchy began an apprenticeship at the couture house of Jacques Fath, whilst studying at the Ecole des Beaux-Arts in Paris. Upon graduation, he became a design assistant to Lucien Lelong, later working for other illustrious designers, including Robert Piguet and then Elsa Schiaparelli, where he honed his dressmaking skills for four years and designed 'separates' for the Schiaparelli boutique. Givenchy opened his couture house in 1951 at 3, avenue George V, opposite Balenciaga. The two couturiers were said to be in contact every day. In 1956, to prevent piracy of their designs, a practice that was rampant throughout Europe and the United States, they announced that they would not show their collections to the press until the day before the delivery date to clients and buyers. Balenciaga assisted Givenchy in finding his design niche — glorious evening gowns, cocktail dresses and youthful daywear suitable for post-war lifestyles.

The year 1954 was an important one for Givenchy: he established his fragrance business and created his first designs for Audrey Hepburn. Givenchy became a household name after the actress wore his specially designed creations in such films as *Sabrina* (1954), *Funny Face* (1957) and *Breakfast at Tiffany's* (1961). His clothes found great favour with many of the world's fashion leaders, including Gloria and Dolores Guinness, Jacqueline Kennedy, Barbara 'Babe' Paley, the Duchess of Windsor and Princess Grace, who wore many of his designs in the 1960s.

In an attempt to compete with the force of the London fashion scene at this time, Givenchy expanded his business in the late 1960s and '70s to include women's ready-to-wear clothing and a line of menswear. He sold his company to the French luxury conglomerate LVMH in 1988 but continued to serve as head designer until his retirement in 1995. John Galliano was his successor, designing for the house for a year, followed by Alexander McQueen. In 2001 McQueen resigned and Julien MacDonald was chosen as the artistic director of the company, designing both the haute couture and women's ready-to-wear collections, with Ozwald Boateng at the head of the men's collection. Riccardo Tisci was then appointed chief designer of collections in 2005. *S.E.S*

Princess Grace chose many Givenchy designs throughout the 1960s, including this luxurious evening gown from 1967 worn to the *Bal de la Rose* at the Monte Carlo opera on 8 February 1970 (right). Givenchy also supplied several outfits for official engagements, including the green ensemble worn to the White House in 1961 (see p.82), a textured silk cloqué dress and jacket worn to the celebrations for Monaco's National Day in November 1962 (top left) and a creamy white woollen suit with decorated buttons. The last was worn during the prince and princess's 1961 visit to Ireland, and also to a Red Cross event in 1962; the princess is photographed here with Mr John MacAulay, president of the Canadian Red Cross Society (bottom left).

Grace Kelly Style

THE PRINCESS

Her Serene Highness Princess Grace of Monaco devoted herself to her new life. Primarily focused on her husband and children, she also worked hard to establish roots in her adopted country, using her celebrity and considerable drive in support of her husband's principality, as well as charitable and cultural causes. The princess's classic American glamour now incorporated European haute couture and fine jewellery, but she remained faithful to the style she had established for herself as an actress and which she had made famous as the 'Grace Kelly Look'. Even as she gradually and gracefully ceded the fashion lead to others, Princess Grace remained one of the most admired women in the world. During the more than 26 years she was Princess of Monaco, her public and private lives and her style were endlessly dissected, but the princess, drawing on the unique qualities that had already characterized her as an actress, retained her regal grace.

Previous page. To commemorate the royal couple's 10th wedding anniversary, Princess Grace was photographed by Howell Conant in 1966 in a dress by Marc Bohan of Christian Dior. Made of ivory silk in a pattern of stylized leaves outlined in gold lamé, it came with a matching long double-breasted evening coat.

Left. By November 1956 Princess Grace was obviously pregnant. At this ceremony in Monaco marking the arrival of the USS *Constellation* she wears a tailored suit with a gently flared jacket and the Cartier diamond brooch in the shape of a poodle that was one of her favourite pieces of jewellery.

Right. In anticipation of the royal birth in Monaco, *Paris Match* featured a cover of the pregnant Princess Grace wearing a high-waisted chiffon gown by Dior, with a diamond rivière necklace by Cartier.

When Prince Rainier and Princess Grace returned from their honeymoon in early June 1956, rumours immediately began that the princess was expecting a baby. The first American visitor the new princess entertained was the designer Helen Rose, and some declared that she must have come specifically to create maternity frocks for the royal mother-to-be.[1] The couple's visit to Paris in July also fuelled speculation that the princess had gone to buy her pregnancy wardrobe, although she said she was there just to see 'all the wonderful tempting things', and ordered several non-maternity garments after a private preview of Lanvin-Castillo's autumn/winter collection.[2]

After Princess Grace's pregnancy was eventually confirmed on 2 August, her maternity wear continued to fascinate. The costume designer Edith Head weighed in on the subject, recommending pretty, soft shades such as pale blue chiffon and suggesting that this specialized wardrobe should be purchased from a Paris fashion house, noting the princess's preference for Dior.[3] Whether this advice was transmitted to Princess Grace is unknown, but at least one of her evening dresses exactly matched her friend's prescription: she was featured on the cover of *Paris Match* on 26 January 1957 wearing a pastel chiffon maternity evening gown by Dior, together with a tiara, glasses and long white gloves. At a time when expectant women had little fashion choice beyond the unbecoming yet ubiquitous maternity smock, Princess Grace attracted international attention with her 'fashion-wise maternity wardrobe'.[4] Her simply styled dark dresses and tailored suits and use of bright scarves and hats to draw attention to her face and away from her figure were cited as excellent models for expectant mothers who wanted to be glamorous.[5]

During the autumn of 1956 Prince Rainier and Princess Grace made a six-week trip to the United States. They took full advantage of what the princess said

were the better prices and variety of American infants' clothing — in fact, they bought so many baby clothes that Prince Rainier joked they had enough for six babies.[6] These garments included some by the renowned American designer Charles James, who applied his distinctive and innovative fashion approach to an infants' line after the birth of his son.[7] Princess Grace bought both boys' things in blue and girls' wear in pink, as well as lots of clothes in yellow, a colour she said she had always loved.[8] She also knitted some baby garments herself.

Admiration for the style of the former Grace Kelly continued: in early January 1957 she was named on the Best-Dressed List for 1956.[9] A few weeks later, the princess gave birth to a daughter, Princess Caroline. The royal baby was warmly welcomed by her parents and by the wider world, where she was already a style setter: her layette included so much yellow that she was said to have popularized this gender-neutral colour, and sunny yellow was dubbed 'princess yellow' in her honour.[10]

In April 1957 the first anniversary of the royal wedding engendered reports of the former star's happiness as a wife and mother, and noted her dedication to her new role as Princess of Monaco. Already earning great admiration for her public role, Princess Grace was said to be 'setting a new fashion in royalty'.[11] Her wardrobe now included more formal daywear and numerous evening gowns, since she dressed for dinner every night, but otherwise she wore the same kind of simple clothes she had always preferred, such as wool dresses and sweaters and skirts. Private showings from couturiers such as Lanvin-Castillo and Dior, both of whom sent models to Monaco each season, enabled the princess to select her wardrobe in privacy and at leisure. The garments and accessories she chose did not remain private for long, however, since her fashion influence remained strong.

Interest in sunglasses as fashion accessories had surged in the summer of 1956 thanks to the myriad wedding-related photographs of the royal bride wearing dark glasses, and the sunglasses boom accelerated the following summer, with a new demand for large, unornamented masculine-like styles directly inspired by 'Princess Grace Kelly'.[12] Eyewear continued to be one of the princess's signature accessories. She was credited with starting the early 1960s vogue for very tiny gold-rimmed glasses, and her example helped make glasses so popular that by the late 1960s even some women with perfect vision adopted them.[13] As a founder-member of the 'sunglasses set' (which also included Jacqueline Kennedy and Brigitte Bardot), the princess promoted dark glasses as a suitable fashion accessory for night, indoors and in the rain — it was said she even wore them at a ball.[14] By 1980 Princess Grace had an extensive 'wardrobe' of glasses, including about 45 pairs created by the celebrated spectacle designer Oliver Goldsmith of London, allowing her to be 'thoroughly color co-ordinated'.[15]

For her new royal role, Princess
Grace required a wardrobe of
formal daywear and evening
gowns for frequent official visits
and social events. Here the royal
couple arrive at the sporting club
in Monaco for the annual Red
Cross Ball, on 20 July 1957.

The accessory most associated with Princess Grace is the Hermès handbag that became known as the 'Kelly' bag. Oversized handbags shaped like mail pouches or briefcases were popular by the mid-1950s, due in part to Grace Kelly's use in *Rear Window* of a Mark Cross case-shaped bag and to her prominent use in private life of the padlocked Hermès bag, modelled after a saddlebag and made by the Parisian company since the 1930s. She was often photographed wielding one — as a star at the Cannes Film Festival in 1955, at her engagement announcement, on her departure from New York, during the pre-wedding festivities in Monaco and on her honeymoon.[16] Thanks to this publicity, by the late summer and autumn of 1956 replicas of the large bag — already called the Grace Kelly handbag — were bestsellers in the United States and London. By 1960 the authentic and expensive 'Kelly' bag was a well-known status symbol, and both the price and the length of the waiting list to buy one have continued to increase.

Princess Grace's choice of hats also continued to make headlines. Some palace insiders thought that, as an American, she took too long to understand court headwear etiquette. Others, however, claimed that the princess had done more for hats than any other woman in the past 20 years:[17] the American millinery trade association, for example, presented her — 'the best chapeaued

Left. Princess Grace continued to inspire fashions in accessories, including spectacles. This photograph, taken in Lausanne, Switzerland, in 1958, shows her in her trademark sunglasses and with the Hermès bag that had been renamed after its most famous fan.

woman in the world' — with their first annual Golden Hat Award in October 1957.[18]

By the end of the summer of 1957 there was speculation that the Princess of Monaco was expecting again, prompted by her reported purchase of maternity dresses from Lanvin-Castillo,[19] and the news was officially announced that September. A month later, a poll revealed that Princess Grace was the leading role model for American teenage girls, with 20 per cent admiring the former film star turned princess and mother compared to 14 per cent each for Queen Elizabeth II and Marilyn Monroe.[20] The princess's understated style also won praise internationally: in December 1957 a British newspaper, the *Daily Mirror*, commended Princess Grace, then on a private visit to London, for the modesty of her demeanour and her good sense, noting with approval her lack of flamboyance and fuss.[21]

To the great joy of his parents and the Monégasque people, Princess Grace gave birth to a male heir, Prince Albert II, in March 1958. While the princess was now finding motherhood more consuming and rewarding than ever, her style remained a focus of interest. In November 1958 the *New York Times* ran a brief announcement with the sole purpose of informing readers that Princess Grace had ordered Balenciaga suits and Maggy Rouff evening dresses for a forthcoming visit to the United States.[22] On the trip, the princess attended a New York charity ball and attracted a 'barrage of adulation' in her ultra-feminine pink Rouff gown with dramatic sequin-studded net fichu and a dazzling display of diamonds.[23] Whether she wore simple or magnificent clothes, *Look* magazine declared in 1959, Princess Grace had an 'unerring eye for the appropriate', and her selections enhanced both her beauty and her station.[24] Experts agreed, and, after a two-year maternity hiatus, she was on that year's Best-Dressed List.

Princess Grace's approach to style still showed common sense. In 1960 she told a journalist that, while she sometimes brought in a hairdresser from Monte Carlo for special occasions, ordinarily she styled her own hair. She noted that she still wore many of her American clothes, but also ordered from European stores and designers and visited Paris at least once each autumn to buy winter clothes. Asked about her clothing budget, she said that she kept within a certain margin, 'but the truth is I don't spend a great deal of money on clothes. There are other things I'd rather use it for.' She was often asked to donate her old dresses and gowns, but, she said, 'I am not eager to give away my things just because they're worn. I keep my things longer than most people.'[25]

Given her wish to keep old favourites in her expanding wardrobe — she sometimes had to change clothes four times in one day for different functions — Princess Grace needed storage space. She objected to the original renovation plan for the royal family's country villa, Roc Agel, since there was not a single closet — 'as you can imagine, to an American girl that was a dreadful thing'. To the consternation of the architect, she insisted on starting afresh, designing the house around the closets.[26]

Prince Rainier was said to love to see his wife beautifully dressed, and had definite ideas about her clothing. 'If the prince doesn't like what I choose, I don't buy it', Princess Grace said eight months after their marriage.[27] The prince, who preferred blue and soft shades on his wife, often went shopping with her; when they attended the Paris collections, she said that he counterbalanced her innate thriftiness, urging her to buy more than she originally intended. The princess noted that her husband had extremely good taste in clothes, instinctively liking the most expensive things without knowing their cost, which she thought 'a delightful quality in a man'.[28] Prince Rainier also surprised his wife with dresses he had

Above. In the winter of 1958 Prince Rainier and Princess Grace visited the United States amidst considerable press attention. She was photographed at a charity ball in New York in a very romantic gown in pale pink silk by Maggy Rouff. Post-maternity clothes such as this put her back on the Best-Dressed List (see also p.68).

Below. For informal occasions,
Princess Grace often wore
comfortable dresses or skirt suits,
with jewellery adding a touch of
individuality. As illustrated by
this photograph, taken during a
family visit to Florida in 1963,
when 'off-duty' she often dressed
her children in equally smart
but practical clothes.

chosen for her.[29] According to the princess, even her young children played a part in her wardrobe: in 1960 she related that Caroline, then aged 3, and Albert, then 22 months, usually came to play with her in the morning and often made a game out of helping her select her clothes.[30]

Princess Grace considered her first duty to be that of wife and mother, and, in contrast to traditional royal mothers, made it a priority to spend time with her children. She also took her role as Princess of Monaco very seriously. In addition to official visits to foreign countries and other duties that supported her husband as head of state or promoted the interests of the principality, she was very active in charitable work. In 1958, soon after the birth of Prince Albert, she assumed chairmanship of Monaco's Red Cross. She became deeply involved in cultural, arts and social service organizations of all kinds, and her commitment went beyond the merely ceremonial. She apparently even found a new use for her signature white gloves: after a hospital visit in 1958, a nurse revealed the thoroughness of the princess's interest and inspection: 'She pokes into closets and looks under beds. She wears a pair of white gloves. If the gloves are dirty when she leaves we really hear about it.'[31] While her family and new position kept the princess fully occupied, she did harbour hopes of acting again; but although great excitement greeted the palace's announcement in 1962 that she would film Hitchcock's mystery *Marnie* during a family trip to the United States, the Monégasque people disapproved, and, citing timing difficulties, the plan was abandoned.

Left. In May 1961 the royal couple visited the White House for an informal lunch with President and Mrs Kennedy. The meeting of the two style leaders was avidly discussed by fashion columnists at the time.

The Best-Dressed List of 1960 elevated Princess Grace to the Fashion Hall of Fame, a distinction introduced two years before for those who had been on the list three or more times. That same year, Jacqueline Kennedy, the wife of the president-elect, appeared on the list for the first time, premiering at the top; when she became First Lady in January 1961, the 'Jackie Look' swept America. In May 1961 the Monégasque royal couple visited the White House for an informal luncheon; the meeting of the two style 'goddesses' created what one fashion columnist imagined was 'a red hot moment'.[32] The First Lady was dressed in a sleeveless black sheath dress with a three-strand pearl necklace tucked inside the high neckline. Princess Grace wore a vivid green Givenchy dress and fringed bolero jacket, elbow-length white kid gloves, gold jewellery and a white petalled turban hat by the milliner Jean Barthet. (Although the hat, which covered most of her hair, was deemed flattering, some speculated that it also served to cover her fashionable but troublesome 'artichoke' hair-do.[33]) The two women chatted about their children — each had a young daughter named Caroline — and the press noted other similarities between them. They were both young,

Right. A detail of the fine wool sleeveless dress with tie belt, and matching jacket edged with fringe, by Givenchy, which she wore to the White House.

slim, beautiful and rich; both were married to good-looking, powerful men; and both were extremely potent fashion influences, having sold 'thousands of fashions as surely as if they had stood behind the counter with sales books and pencils'.[34]

Reporters contrasted Princess Grace's 'cool beauty' to the 'vivacious beauty' of Jacqueline Kennedy, whose fashion influence spread the following month when she visited France with her husband.[35] The two women topped *Time* magazine's list of nine reigning beauties in 1962, hailed as 'a new and lively generation' of effective royal women and first ladies renowned for their 'charm, taste, tact — and looks'.[36] To some European observers, Princess Grace and Jacqueline Kennedy epitomized a particularly American style of beauty. In her book of 1964, *Elegance*, Geneviève Dariaux, *directrice* of the Parisian couture house of Nina Ricci, praised their style — characterized by faultless grooming, simple ensembles in perfect taste and harmony and a youthful air — as eliciting 'the admiration of every man', as well as 'the envy of other women'.[37]

Princess Grace's approach to fashion in the early 1960s was elegant, tasteful and appropriate, but not adventurous. In 1963 her former beau Oleg Cassini maintained that she had taken stock of herself and, realizing she was most interested in being proper, had accordingly selected subdued rather than dramatic clothing.[38] The princess's clothes were sometimes too conservative and unimaginative for fashion insiders: when she visited London in January 1963, the *Daily Express*'s fashion writer made international headlines by sniping at nearly everything she wore to go window-shopping, from a dated turban, over-long hemline and low-heeled shoes to her glasses, stockings and 'insignificant' gloves.[39] The following month, the princess narrated an American television special, 'A Look at Monaco', with an on-camera wardrobe that included a Balenciaga suit, Lanvin evening gown and Givenchy dress, giving 'arm-chair fashion critics' the opportunity to judge her sartorial merits for themselves.[40]

In February 1965 the royal couple happily added a third child, Princess Stéphanie, to their young family. In an era when many mothers relied on bottle feeding, Princess Grace, who ardently supported La Leche League, breastfed each child for two months; she explained that she would have continued longer, but, like many other contemporary mothers, she had to get back to work. Since she did not think nursing mothers should diet, she inevitably gained weight. Three months after Stéphanie's birth, the princess arrived in New York wearing a nine-year-old Ben Zuckerman coat from her trousseau. 'It's still just as good a coat as ever', she asserted matter-of-factly. 'I'm a little overweight since my baby, and it fits.'[41] Although she managed to lose weight after each pregnancy, her figure caused her increasing concern.

In 1963 Princess Grace narrated an American television special, 'A Look at Monaco'. One of the ensembles she chose for the filming in November 1962 was a suit designed by Balenciaga that used the hand-woven green tweed she had received as a gift in Clifden, Connemara, on a state visit to Ireland in June 1961.

Left. Throughout the 1960s Princess Grace wore increasingly elaborate coiffeurs created by the Parisian hairdresser Alexandre. She often wore a 'postiche' or extra braids of false hair, as seen in this hair creation photographed at the Red Cross Ball on 9 August 1968.

While she remained true to her own fashion sense and continued to wear her favourite clothes, Princess Grace nonetheless embraced some of the new spirit of the mid-1960s. At Saks Fifth Avenue in New York she 'went mad' for wildly coloured floral mesh nylon stockings.[42] Although many were shocked when the House of Dior sold inexpensive silk dresses stamped all over with the designer's famous name — an unexpected conceit at the time — the princess snapped up half a dozen in different colours.[43] Princess Grace also purchased a dress from Yves Saint Laurent's revolutionary autumn/winter 1965 collection. Inspired by the work of Dutch painter Piet Mondrian, Saint Laurent's young and exhilarating collection won raves reviews and that August was hailed as 'the most exciting thing in Paris'.[44] Princess Grace bought a geometric 'crusader' dress of black bands dividing up white with a red block on the left shoulder — said to be the hottest number in the group.[45] When she wore it to distribute Christmas presents to Monégasque children, she fastened a favourite brooch in the shape of a poodle on the red block in place of the designer's original Maltese jewel pin.

In the 1960s, a decade known for adventurous hair, Princess Grace made news with her hairstyles and was a celebrated client of the famed Parisian hairdresser Alexandre, known for his innovative and extreme coiffeurs. Her short cut was usually simply styled during the day, but she sometimes wore a long 'fall' or 'postiche' to augment her hair — one of the first fashion leaders to do so — explaining: 'It's fun, and covers a multitude of sins.'[46] For evening galas, all manner of faux chignons and braids could be used to transform her hair into elaborate and fanciful creations. The princess was on the list of 'Ten Best Coiffured Women' in 1962 and 1967, and in

Far right. Although Princess Grace felt ambivalent about some of the more daring designs of the 1960s, she bought a dress from Yves Saint Laurent's revolutionary 'Mondrian' collection of autumn/ winter 1965. Here she hosts the annual Christmas party for children at the Princely Palace of Monaco, accessorizing the dress with her favourite brooch of a poodle.

Right. A detail showing the craftsmanship of Princess Grace's wool jersey 'crusader' dress by Saint Laurent.

1968 was selected as one of the first three women on a 'Heads of Fame' list.[47]

Fashion in the late 1960s increasingly favoured youth, egalitarianism and diversity, and the fads of 'young swingers' did not appeal to the princess. In April 1966 she called the current Paris collections 'just awful', and fretted: 'They can't do this to us women much longer.'[48] Her conservatism pleased some, including the British press, which unanimously applauded the dress and hat she wore to Royal Ascot in 1966 as 'bang out of the royal tradition and all the better for it'.[49] Princess Grace articulated her objections to the new modes: 'I don't like anything too obvious — sex or makeup or a way of dressing. I prefer something that's understated; that leaves a little to the imagination.'[50] At a charity fashion show in 1968 she clapped politely for a see-through evening pyjama outfit by Patou, but said: 'I don't see myself wearing that.'[51] She did not like very short skirts. 'After all, who has pretty knees?' she asked in 1965,[52] and later commented: 'I think they're fun on young girls, but I have never thought I was the mini-skirt type.'[53] (By early 1970, however, the practical princess was worried that if hemlines dropped suddenly she would not be able to get much wear out of the Chanels she had bought the previous autumn.[54])

While Princess Grace was generally conservative and committed to upholding the dignity of her husband's position, she dispensed with some centuries-old protocol. Women had always been required to wear hats to lunch at the Monégasque palace, but, when millinery went out of fashion in the late 1960s, the princess relaxed this rule, to the consternation of traditionalists.[55] Prince Rainier continued to disapprove of women wearing trousers in the palace well into the 1970s, however, and Princess Grace shared his reservations, supporting restaurants and hotels that banned trousers on women, noting that few looked really chic and elegant in them.[56] She wore trousers in the country or for casual activities, but believed that clothes 'should make a woman look like a woman'. On the rare occasions that she wore dressier versions,

Below. For Royal Ascot in 1966, Princess Grace wore a shift dress embroidered with three-dimensional flowers by Marie-Thérèse of Nice, one of the dressmakers she patronized in the Monégasque region. Her wide-brimmed, 'off-the-face'-style straw hat was appreciated by the British press.

Right. In September 1967
Princess Grace attended a
masked ball at the Rezzonico
Palace in Venice, wearing a
favourite white lace gown by
Marc Bohan for Christian Dior
(spring/summer 1966), with
an embellished 'domino' cloak
and an improvised gold mask.
Her fancy dress costumes
were often designed by theatre
designer André Levasseur,
who had previously worked
for Christian Dior.

'I keep my blouse soft and feminine and select trousers that are graceful, and flatter the figure rather than expose it.'[57]

Princess Grace brought her well-known glamour to numerous charity and celebratory balls, and also attended a number of fancy-dress balls in the mid- to late 1960s that recreated some of the romance of past times. At Monte Carlo's centenary costume ball in 1966, she sported an enormous peach crinoline and masses of curls, and at a 1900-style ball in 1968 she was said to be at her most beautiful in a black net gown with gold embroidery and an aigrette-spiked hairstyle.[58] Exotic balls allowed for fun with fantastic dress, even if sometimes improvised or inconvenient: when her mask failed to arrive in time for a Venetian masquerade in 1967, the princess pasted sequins around her eyes and draped a gold mesh necklace over her nose, while in 1969 her towering gold-wire belled headdress for a Monte Carlo ball required that she travel the short distance on the floor of a van (see p.98).[59]

Princess Grace celebrated her 40th birthday in November 1969 with a Scorpio-themed ball. Despite growing older, which came as a great jolt to her, she continued to be regarded as one of the era's great beauties, and observers credited her not only with elegance, dignity and charm, but also a unique simplicity and an aura of serenity.[60] While she had never thought of herself as pretty, claiming that she had been too bland to be beautiful when she was younger, she felt that she had improved her looks by learning to make the best of her good points and hide bad ones.[61] 'It takes time to establish your own style', she explained in 1970. 'Now for the past 10 years I have felt truly at ease with fashion.'[62] While the princess described herself as 'fussy and particular about what I wear and uncomfortable if it doesn't fit quite right', she did not place too much emphasis on clothes.[63] 'I have learned to say "no" to a dress, however pretty, because you know it won't give you value as a person', she said. 'I think it is important to see the person first and the clothes afterward.'[64] She believed that a woman's personality should dominate that of the designer; since it was the designer's job to enhance the wearer, she disliked those who plastered their clothes with recognizable signals.[65]

Explaining how she selected her wardrobe in the early 1970s, the princess said: 'Twice a year, I think what clothes I will need for the coming months. Then I usually ask to see some sketches from the Paris couturiers.'[66] A number of designers knew her measurements so she could shop by mail, and, although she attended charity or gala fashion shows, she did not usually see collections live. Princess Grace considered Marc Bohan of Dior her standby,[67] believing that the house knew her style, her needs and what would be appropriate. She also liked Yves Saint Laurent, Chanel and Madame Grès, and was a loyal customer of dressmakers in Monaco and Nice, and often half-designed clothes with them or asked them to make up a special fabric she had brought in.[68]

Princess Grace was not interested in conforming to every dictate of modern fashion. 'As I get older,' she admitted, 'I get lazier . . . and my clothes must be comfortable.'[69] She nevertheless felt that her clothes were sometimes unfairly criticized, and was distressed when the press accused her of trying to upstage Princess Anne at her

Left. In the 1970s both Prince Rainier and Princess Grace disapproved of women wearing trousers in the palace, but the practical princess did wear them for walking in the country and for casual activities, as seen here in 1973.

Above. Princess Grace, here on the cover of British *Vogue* on 1 March 1972 at the age of 42, continued to be considered one of the world's most beautiful women.

Right. In the late 1960s a series of spectacular fancy dress balls were highlights of the international jet set's social calendar. In 1968, to a costume ball inaugurating the European room at the Monte Carlo Casino, the princess wore a '1900 style' black net gown embroidered with gold thread that was said to set off her beauty. It was made by the Nice fashion house Gilbert Dublin, after a design by André Levasseur, who designed elaborate sets for the Monte Carlo balls.

wedding in 1973 by wearing a white ensemble by Dior's Marc Bohan.[70] By the late 1970s her figure was no longer sylph-like, and she was favouring turbans and floppy hats, flowing caftans and dresses with high collars, long sleeves and flounced skirts that some thought matronly.[71] The Princess of Monaco remained renowned for her beauty, however, and at 46 was on *Harper's Bazaar's* list of America's ten most beautiful women.[72]

In the mid-1970s Princess Grace, together with Stéphanie, moved to Paris part-time to be with the teenage Princess Caroline, a student at the Institute d'Etudes Politiques. Caroline was also making news for beauty and style sense, and at the age of 18 was named on the Best-Dressed List of 1974. She was slightly taller than Princess Grace, but confessed to raiding her mother's wardrobe.[73] Both princesses shared a taste for Dior, and Marc Bohan designed ensembles for them for the civil and religious ceremonies when Caroline married Philippe Junot in 1978.

As her children got older in the late 1970s, Princess Grace's public role expanded. She derived great satisfaction from a series of poetry readings and narrated a documentary about the Kirov ballet school. She continued to promote the arts, including working on

In March 1981 Princess Grace met Lady Diana Spencer, soon to become the Princess of Wales, at a benefit gala for the Royal Opera House in London. Princess Grace is dressed by Yves Saint Laurent, while Lady Diana wears a dress by the British designers David and Elizabeth Emanuel.

behalf of the Princess Grace Foundation of Monaco, which she had established in 1964 to support local artisans and aspiring young dancers and musicians. She spearheaded the drive to build a theatre in Monaco, and served on the board of 20th Century Fox. The princess's lifelong love of flowers had led her to found an annual flower show and the Garden Club of Monaco in the 1960s; this love was now expressed though her dried flower collages, which were exhibited in Paris and adapted for household linen designs by a manufacturer, and in her 1980 publication *My Book of Flowers*.

As she entered her fifties, Princess Grace seemed to be finding new outlets for her talents and was generally regarded as the ideal gracious royal princess. In March 1981, wearing a crown of braids and a purple Yves Saint Laurent gown, she participated in a benefit gala for the Royal Opera House in London, the first public appearance of Lady Diana Spencer after her engagement to Prince Charles. Only too familiar with the maelstrom of media attention after nearly 25 years as Princess of Monaco, she went out of her way to befriend the future Princess of Wales, dazzling but overwhelmed in a low-cut strapless black dress.

On 13 September 1982 Princess Grace and her daughter Stéphanie were driving from Roc Agel to the palace; the back seat of the car was covered by dresses she was taking to be altered, so she waved away her usual chauffeur and got into the driver's seat herself. On the twisting mountain road, she suffered a small stroke and the car plunged off the road. Stéphanie was slightly hurt, but Princess Grace died of her injuries the following day. While her life was tragically cut short, the innate elegance and unmistakable style she showed as an actress, bride and princess continue to be remembered and admired.

Prince Rainier and Princess Grace celebrated their 25th wedding anniversary in April 1981. For this photograph to mark the occasion, the princess wore a white chiffon dress by Marc Bohan of Christian Dior and jewellery by Van Cleef & Arpels.

CRISTÓBAL BALENCIAGA

Cristóbal Balenciaga (1895–1972) is the most famous Spanish couturier of all time and a legendary figure in fashion, known for his innovative designs and the supreme quality of his tailoring. Taught to sew by his mother, he became apprenticed to a tailor in the fashionable city of Donostia-San Sebastián, where he opened his first boutique in either 1914 or 1915. In 1934 he launched another fashion house in the centre of Madrid. Eisa, a shortened form of his mother's maiden name, opened in Barcelona the following year. Two years later Balenciaga emigrated to Paris via London, escaping the political tensions that would lead to the Spanish Civil War. He opened the house of Balenciaga at 10, avenue George V in 1937, in the centre of French luxury and couture production. The business expanded steadily, and by 1955 there was a total of ten workshops producing Balenciaga's beautifully structured suits and evening wear.

The couturier took inspiration from his homeland; some of the simple forms he favoured, such as circular shifts and simple tunics, were derived from matadors' capes and Spanish clerical dress. His designs were made in luxurious fabrics in dark passionate colours — black, brilliant red, purple, shades of grey and earth tones — while his evening wear was often embellished with heavy embroidery or black lace. Balenciaga based his design philosophy on utilizing the inherent qualities of fabric, which led to innovative tailored, draped and sculpted forms, such as the 'sack' dress of 1952 that prefigured the simple shift dresses of 1960s youth fashions. Balenciaga's clients included members of European royal families, including Princess Grace and Queen Fabiola of Belgium, actresses such as Ava Gardner, and very wealthy women like Mona Bismarck and Barbara Rockefeller. Balenciaga mentored many young designers such as André Courrèges, Emanuel Ungaro and Oscar de la Renta, and received the Légion d'honneur for services to the French fashion industry. In 1968 he retired and closed his house in Paris, remarking 'This is a dog's life'. The Eisa boutique closed in 1969 and Balenciaga died in Jávea, Spain, in 1972. Currently, Gucci Group and the designer Nicolas Ghesquière own the brand and archive, and have made the house one of the most forward-thinking and creative forces in the industry. *S.E.S*

From the late 1950s until his couture house closed in 1968, Balenciaga provided Princess Grace with supremely tailored suits and dresses and some spectacular evening gowns. She wore this white silk sheath dress with an ornately embroidered bolero jacket to a gala at the Hôtel de Paris during an official visit to the French capital in October 1959.

MARC BOHAN

Marc Bohan (b.1926) is best known for his work over three decades as artistic director of Christian Dior. He was introduced to the world of fashion at a young age by his mother, a milliner in Paris. He first worked for the fashion house Jean Patou, providing sketches in 1945, and then became assistant designer at Piguet in 1946. Christian Dior, Pierre Balmain and Hubert de Givenchy had also gained experience at Piguet's house. After military service in 1948, Bohan joined Edward Molyneux as a design assistant in 1949. Bohan then established his own short-lived couture house in 1953. In 1954 he finally settled at Patou, where he designed sophisticated and wearable dresses such as the 'Paris' dress, a black crêpe frock with boat neck and a broad sash that draped under the bust, enhancing the neckline. After four years at Patou, in 1957, he was called to Christian Dior London to design the ready-to-wear collection, also supervising the Christian Dior–New York label. He was asked to become artistic director of Dior after Yves Saint Laurent's departure in 1960.

Bohan presented his first couture collection for Dior on 26 January 1961. His 'Slim Line' collection of little suits, slightly flared at the hem, and chiffon dresses in rich colours was a huge success; Elizabeth Taylor ordered 12 garments. The light, feminine designs echoed Christian Dior's aesthetic but brought in a new sense of freedom. Bohan's collections represented the energy of the 1960s, including contemporary yet elegant designs that appealed not only to existing clientele but also to younger women. He designed a total of 57 haute couture shows from 1961 to 1989, adapting to trends and creating definitive looks with culottes, pinafore dresses, coloured tights, maxicoats and caftans, to mention only a few examples. Under his leadership, in 1967 the ready-to-wear label 'Miss Dior' and the 'Baby Dior' range of clothes for children were launched, and in 1970 a line of Christian Dior clothes for men.

Bohan's 29 years at the helm of Dior made it one of the most profitable brands in the fashion industry, and his designs were worn by women in all fields of culture and politics, such as Jacqueline Kennedy (who for state reasons had Bohan's designs copied by Oleg Cassini), Sophia Loren, Nancy Reagan, Isabelle Adjani and the Duchess of Windsor, as well as Princesses Grace and Caroline of Monaco. In 1983 and 1988 Bohan was awarded the De d'Or (Golden Thimble) Award. After three decades at Dior, Bohan left to design for the house of Norman Hartnell in 1990. *S.E.S*

Princess Grace was a great patron of Christian Dior, especially during Marc Bohan's directorship. On 7 November 1967 she opened the Baby Dior shop wearing a Christian Dior suit (bottom right). Princess Grace was particularly fond of the 'Bayadère' dress (spring/summer 1967; bottom left; see also p.86). She sometimes wore Bohan's opulent dresses to costume balls, with appropriately themed accessories, as seen at the *Dîner des Têtes*, at the Monte Carlo Casino, on 17 March 1969 (top right). Marc Bohan also dressed Princess Caroline, seen here with her mother at the Red Cross Ball in 1973 (top left).

GABRIELLE CHANEL

Chanel became one of the most well-known design brands of the twentieth century. Gabrielle or 'Coco' Chanel (1883–1971) began her career in fashion as a milliner, and in 1910 rented commercial premises on rue Cambon, Paris, where the fashion house is still located. She presented her first fashion collections in 1913 at the holiday resort of Deauville on the Normandy coast. The outbreak of the First World War a year later encouraged wealthy people to stay in Deauville, where women purchased Chanel's inconspicuous and adaptable clothing that suited their increasingly active lifestyles.

In 1917 Chanel created her first couture collection, which demonstrated her utilitarian but luxurious house style. Taking inspiration from the tailoring and sportswear worn by her friend the Duke of Westminster, and using fabrics such as jersey and tweed, she reinterpreted blazers, waistcoats and shirts as desirable garments for women. Her premises on the rue Cambon expanded to include numbers 27, 29 and 31 during the early 1920s. In 1922 her first perfume, Chanel No.5, was launched. The sale of her various perfumes sustained her financially throughout the Second World War.

Chanel is often credited with inventing the little black dress. She challenged convention by wearing lots of jewellery during the daytime, as well as mixing costume jewellery and real jewels together, using them to decorate the body rather than flaunt wealth. In the 1920s Chanel designed costumes for the Ballets Russes, for avant-garde French films and, for a short time, for MGM studios. By 1930, despite the Depression, the house had approximately 4,000 employees, making it one of the largest couture houses in France. Chanel closed her business during the Second World War, although she remained in Paris, later moving to Switzerland.

In February 1954, now in her seventies, Chanel made her famous 'comeback', presenting her first post-war collection. Her unpretentious suits and dresses, constructed in chunky woollen tweeds or jerseys, featured bold braid and gilt chain trim as well as functional pockets. Distinctive handbags with gold chains and quilting and sling-back shoes with contrasting toe caps completed the look. These became enduring trademarks of the Chanel style, and, reworked each season, attracted high-profile clients in the late 1950s and '60s such as Jacqueline Kennedy and Princess Grace. Chanel died in 1971 whilst arranging her spring/summer collection. Karl Lagerfeld has been the chief designer since 1983 and his interpretations of Chanel's signature designs have ensured that they remain relevant and commercially successful in the twenty-first century. *S.E.S*

Princess Grace bought several different Chanel outfits in the 1960s and '70s. She wore them frequently for occasions such as official meetings, family gatherings and private shopping trips, and was photographed in this asymmetrically styled coatdress of pink and green wool tweed in 1971.

YVES SAINT LAURENT

Throughout his prolific career, Yves Saint Laurent (1936–2008) broke new ground in couture, combining impeccable technical production standards with influences from street styles and many different cultures. Born in Algeria, Saint Laurent was a talented artist from childhood and sketched many dress designs for his sister and mother. In 1954 he attended the Ecole de la Chambre Syndicale de la Haute Couture in Paris for three months, and was hired as Christian Dior's assistant. This provided a powerful design apprenticeship, which would last until Dior's sudden death in October 1957. On 15 November, at the age of 21, Saint Laurent was named his successor, becoming the youngest couturier in the world. His first collection, presented in January 1958, won him international fame. This was also the year that he met his partner in business and life, Pierre Bergé.

Drafted into the Algerian forces in 1960, Saint Laurent was replaced at Dior by Marc Bohan. After a brief stint in the army, he was declared unfit for service and hospitalized for nervous depression; illness, drink and drugs plagued the designer throughout his life. In 1961 he opened his own couture house, and his first catwalk show in 1962 introduced designs such as the smock and pea jacket. He produced innovative styles throughout the 1960s, breaking away from the traditions of formality associated with couture. His signature 'Le Smoking' feminine tuxedo of 1966 became a part of many future collections, and Saint Laurent was one of the first couturiers to open a ready-to-wear shop, Rive Gauche, in 1966.

During the 1970s many of his collections created contemporary fashion from eclectic sources inspired by the past or exotic or folk dress, and paid homage to favourite artists and writers. Saint Laurent was frequently commissioned to design for the theatre, film and ballet. In the 1980s exhibitions of his work were held in New York, China and Paris. After 44 years of designing couture, in 2002 Saint Laurent retired and closed the couture part of his business. He passed away in 2008. Stefano Pilati currently designs the ready-to-wear lines for the label. *S.E.S*

Princess Grace was amongst many famous clients who purchased dresses from Yves Saint Laurent's 'Mondrian' collection of 1965 (see p.87). Saint Laurent was to remain an important supplier to the princess's wardrobe, and she wore many of his designs throughout the 1970s, including a brown patterned maxi-coat and matching dress, photographed here in 1970 (bottom right), a black chiffon gown woven with gold lamé spots, photographed with Elizabeth Taylor in 1971 (top left), and a gold lamé tunic and trousers of about 1975 (bottom left). She selected a classic ensemble of layered blue and green chiffon for a poetry reading in 1980 (top right).

MADAME GRÈS

Madame Grès (née Germaine Emilie Krebs, 1903–1993) is best known for her dresses of fluid silk jersey, pleated to fit the body, forming unique, innovative gowns reminiscent of Grecian sculpture. Born in Paris, she originally strove to be a dancer, then later a sculptor, happening on dress design after her parents discouraged her initial plans. At the beginning of the 1930s she was apprenticed to the couture house of Premet, where she changed her first name to Alix. She later moved to the atelier of the couturier Julie Barton, who recognized her talent and renamed the house Alix in her honour. She married the Russian-born painter Serge Anatolievitch Czerefkow in 1937, and became Alix Grès (an anagram of her husband's first name). Anne, her only daughter, was born in 1939. When the war broke out, they fled from Paris; since she could not attend a hairdresser's during her exile, Grès took to wearing a turban, which became her personal mark of style. In 1941 she returned to Paris and opened her own couture house at 1, rue de la Paix, though she had to close the business briefly in 1944.

Towards the end of that year, she was allowed to resume trading and designed the celebrated dress collection that used only blue, white and red, the colours of the French flag.

Madame Grès' business flourished in the 1950s and '60s through licensed products and her new perfume, Cabochard (literally meaning 'pig-headed'), was introduced in 1959. After a trip to India her designs reflected a new 'hippy' aesthetic, and during the mid-1960s she created caftans, capes and pyjamas. Many high-profile women were among her clients, particularly in the 1970s, including Marlene Dietrich, the socialite Nan Kempner, Barbra Streisand and Princess Grace.

In 1972 Grès was elected president of the Chambre Syndicale de la Couture, and four years later she was awarded the De d'Or (Golden Thimble) award. The house was in decline by the 1980s, however; in 1984 Madame Grès sold the business, and in 1986 she was expelled from the Chambre Syndicale for failure to pay her dues. In 1988 she officially retired from couture, and the great 'sculptress' or 'sphinx' of haute couture died quietly five years later in the south of France. *S.E.S*

Princess Grace, with her height and classical beauty, perfected the ability to carry off Grès' innovative, sculptural gowns in taffeta and her more typical fluid jersey ensembles. While being supremely comfortable, these were also appropriate for the princess's official duties, and she accessorized them with jewellery to great effect. She is photographed here by Lord Snowdon in 1972.

Notes

Introduction

1   Gwen Robyns, *Princess Grace* (London, 1976), pp.88–9.

2   Barbara Hulanicki, *From A to Biba* (London, 1983; new edition 2007), p.52.

3   Norman Hartnell, 'Notes on People', interview for *New York Times* (31 December 1976); quoted in Michael Pick,
    Be Dazzled! Norman Hartnell: Sixty Years of Glamour and Fashion (New York, 2007), p.34.

Chapter 1

1   Producer Fred Coe quoted in Isabella Taves, 'The Seven Graces', *McCall's* (January 1955), p.68.

2   Quoted by Erskine Johnson (Newspaper Enterprise Association), *Indiana Evening Gazette* [Pennsylvania] (2 April 1955).

3   E. Head and P. Calistro, *Edith Head's Hollywood* (New York, 1983), pp.108–9. See also David Chierichetti, *Edith Head:
    The Life and Times of Hollywood's Celebrated Costume Designer* (New York, 2003), p.126.

4   R.I.S., 'Her Beauty, Acting Save Film', *Syracuse Herald-Journal* (15 September 1955).

5   Gwen Robyns, *Princess Grace* (London, 1976), p.110.

6   Helen Rose, *The Glamorous World of Helen Rose* (Palm Springs, 1983), p.58.

7   Bob Thomas, 'Hollywood Personalities', *Joplin Globe* (14 January 1954).

8   'Hollywood's Hottest Property', *Life* (26 April 1954), p.117.

9   *Newsweek* (17 May 1954), p.17; Aline Mosby (United Press), 'Grace Is Cinderella in Reverse', *Syracuse Herald-Journal* (20 November 1954).

10   Richard G. Hubler, 'They All Gambled on Grace Kelly', *Redbook* (November 1954), p.108.

11   Head and Calistro, *Edith Head's Hollywood*, p.154.

12   Arlene Dahl, 'Let's Be Beautiful: Grace Kelly Gives Her Views', *San Antonio Light* (2 August 1954).

13   'People Are Talking About . . .', American *Vogue* (1 March 1955), p.130. The actress herself thought that her sizzling love scenes in
    Rear Window and *To Catch A Thief* should have dispelled the notion that she was cool and aloof. Cynthia Lowry (Associated Press),
    'Miss Grace Kelly Quiet Lady From Hollywood', *The Progress* [Clearfield, Pennsylvania] (24 December 1954).

14   'People Are Talking About . . .', p.130.

15   'The Girl in White Gloves', *Time* (31 January 1955), p.46.

16   Ibid.

17   'Express the Grace Kelly Look', *Women's Wear Daily* (8 December 1955).

18   *Monessen Daily Independent* [Pennsylvania] (23 July 1954).

19   Betty Parkinson, '"Grace Kelly Look" for Spring', *Sunday Bulletin* [Philadelphia] (15 January 1956).

20   Lydia Lane, 'Hollywood Beauty: Simplicity Keynotes Grace Kelly', *Oakland Tribune* [California] (21 November 1954).

21   Ibid.

22   Arlene Dahl, 'Let's Be Beautiful: Grace Kelly Gives Her Views', *San Antonio Light* (2 August 1954).

23   Lane, 'Hollywood Beauty'.

24   'Silk and Lace Details are Released by M-G-M Studio', clipping from an unidentified Los Angeles newspaper
    (18 April 1956). Courtesy of Margaret Herrick Library, Academy of Motion Picture Arts and Sciences,
    Beverly Hills, California.

25   Erskine Johnson (Newspaper Enterprise Association), 'Fame Was Grace's Goal: She Reached It Fast',
    Ames Daily Tribune (12 November 1954).

26   'Miss Kelly Talks About Her Clothes', *Philadelphia Inquirer* (5 January 1956).

27   Isabella Traves, 'The Seven Graces', *McCall's* (January 1955), p.71.

28   Paul Crume, 'Everyman's Nice Girl: Miss Kelly Gracing Dallas for Nonce', *Dallas Morning News* (5 September 1955).

29   Associated Press photo caption (5 September 1955). Courtesy of Temple University Urban Archives, Philadelphia.

30   Emily Belser (United Press), 'Today's Fashion High Light', *Daily Courier* [Connellsville, Pennsylvania] (25 November 1955).

31   'Express the Grace Kelly Look', *Women's Wear Daily* (8 December 1955).

32   International News Service, 'Princess Margaret Woman of the Year', *Newport Daily News* [Rhode Island] (24 December 1955).

33   Olga Curtis (International News Service), 'Grace Kelly Ties for First Place among World's Best Dressed Women', *Mansfield News-Journal*
    [Ohio] (5 January 1956). The press called attention to the 'youth movement', which broke with the traditional recognition of older women;
    nine of the fourteen names on the 1955 list were under 35 years of age, including Princess Margaret Rose of Great Britain, born a year after
    Grace Kelly.

34   Edrie Van Dore, 'Grace Kelly Tops Best Dressed List', *Philadelphia Inquirer* (5 January 1956).

Chapter 2

1   Cynthia Cabot, 'Kelly Dress for All', *Philadelphia Inquirer* (19 January 1956). Photographs of the first meeting of Grace Kelly and Prince Rainier were widely printed once their engagement was announced. The same article calls the dress 'the most publicized dress of the season' and suggests that any girl wishing to win her own Prince Charming could sew her own version.

2   The term means 'high belt' in English; the design is derived from a kind of saddlebag. For more details, see p. 78.

3   Alice Connolly, 'Grace Kelly Gets More Notice', *Bridgeport Post* (11 January 1956). After Grace Kelly's engagement, the newly famous dress, although already a season old, was again featured in Branell fashion shows under its new name, 'To Catch a Prince'.

4   'A Most Eligible Prince, a Reigning Movie Queen: A Romance that's Got Everything', *Life* (16 January 1956), p.17.

5   'Grace Kelly Sails in Beige Suit', *Women's Wear Daily* (5 April 1956).

6   Kittie Campbell, 'The Grace Kelly Look: The T-Square Silhouette', *Sunday Bulletin* [Philadelphia] (26 February 1956).

7   Kittie Campbell, 'Playclothes from French Riviera Reflect Grace Kelly Influence', *Evening Bulletin* [Philadelphia] (7 February 1956).

8   Nora W. Martin (International News Service), 'Is Paris Pointing at Grace Kelly?', *Washington Post and Times Herald* (31 January 1956).

9   Nadeane Walker (Associated Press), 'Ladylike Look Has Influence of Paris Styles', *Newport Daily News* [Rhode Island] (3 March 1956).

10   Peggy Massin, 'Paris Models Adopt the Grace Kelly Look', *Evening Bulletin* [Philadelphia] (30 January1956).

11   'And Now Here Comes The Bride', *Life* (9 April 1956), p.45.

12   Cynthia Cabot, '40 Costumes by Top US Designers', *Philadelphia Inquirer* (17 April 1956).

13   Kittie Campbell, 'Grace Goes All-American in Wedding Wardrobe', *Evening Bulletin* [Philadelphia] (17 April 1956).

14   Kittie Campbell, '*SS Constitution* Will Be Floating Fashion Parade', *Evening Bulletin* [Philadelphia] (4 April 1956).

15   'Blue, Beige Dominate Grace Kelly's Trousseau', *Syracuse Post-Standard* (11 April 1956); 'Grace Kelly's Trousseau Is Based on Blue, Beige', *Berkshire Eagle* [Pittsfield, Massachusetts] (6 April 1956); 'Silk Trousseau for Grace', *Lima News* [Ohio] (4 April 1956).

16   Isabel Johns, 'Grace Fully Equipped for Life of Princess', *Boston Daily Globe* (18 April 1956).

17   'Thin Cottons in Grace Kelly's Trousseau', *Women's Wear Daily* (19 March 1956).

18   'Silk Trousseau for Grace', *Lima News* [Ohio] (4 April 1956).

19   Johns, 'Grace Fully Equipped for Life of Princess'.

20   Cabot, '40 Costumes by Top US Designers'.

21   Associated Press, 'Grace Kelly Leaves Today for Wedding', *Gettysburg Times* (5 April 1956).

22   United Press, 'Weeping Grace Sails for Monaco and Life as Royal Princess', *Philadelphia Inquirer* (5 April 1956).

23   '"Don't Let Protocol Get You": John B. Advises Bride-to-Be', *Evening Bulletin* [Philadelphia] (9 April 1956).

24   Henrietta Lowe Terrazas, 'Lowly Tennis Sweater Becomes Glamorous under the Deft Touch of Oleg Cassini', *El Paso Herald-Post* (12 July 1954).

25   'What is Grace Up To?', *Life* (23 April 1956).

26   Associated Press, 'Rainier Miffed by Ambush, Bars All News Photogs', *Philadelphia Inquirer* (14 April 1956). Others reported she wore no hat at all; see Elizabeth Toomey (United Press), 'Prince Rainier Bars Photographers from Palace after Hectic Encounter', *Evening Bulletin* [Philadelphia] (13 April 1956).

27   The Philadelphia Museum of Art has a sleeveless version of the Galanos design, suggesting that perhaps the short sleeves were added to Grace Kelly's trousseau dress to make it more suitable for the future princess.

28   Emily Belser (International News Service), '300 Yards of Lace in Grace's Gown', *Philadelphia Inquirer* (18 April 1956).

29   Ibid.

30   See H. Kristina Haugland, *Grace Kelly: Icon of Style to Royal Bride* (Philadelphia, 2006).

31   David Chierichetti, *Edith Head* (New York, 2003), pp.129–30. Contemporary press accounts do not seem to mention Edith Head's involvement with Princess Grace's going-away outfit.

Chapter 3

1   Emily Belser (International News Service), 'Helen Rose Says Grace Unchanged', *Cedar Rapids Gazette* (11 July 1956).

2   Associated Press, 'Grace Kelly Visits Dressmaker', *Kerrville Times* (12 July 1956); Nora W. Martin (International News Service), 'New Paris Fashions Catch Grace's Fancy', *Washington Post and Times Herald* (26 July 1956).

3   Nora W. Martin (International News Service), 'Hollywood Designer Suggests Paris Wardrobe for Princess', *Kingsport News* (1 September 1956).

4   Eugenia Sheppard, 'Inside Fashion: All-Out War Declared on Maternity Smock', *Corpus Christi Times* [Texas] (10 January 1961).

5   Anne's Reader Exchange, 'Expecting? Then Look Your Best', *Washington Post and Times Herald* (29 April 1958); 'Fashions Go Glamorous for Mothers-To-Be', *Washington Post and Times Herald* (21 July 1957).

6   Norah Littlejohn, 'Princess Grace Tells Her Secrets', *Winnipeg Free Press* (19 January 1957).

7   'Princess' [*sic*] Clothes, Alas, Are Princely', *New York Times* (2 February 1957). See also Elizabeth Ann Coleman, *The Genius of Charles James* (New York, 1982).

8   Olga Curtis (International News Service), 'Princess Grace Plumper, Prettier, Happier, Hopeful', *Elyria Chronicle-Telegram* (5 November 1956).

9   International News Service, 'Mrs William Paley Again Tops Best Dressed List', *Cedar Rapids Gazette* (3 January 1957).

10   Olga Curtis (International News Service), 'Caroline Sets New Trend', *Lowell Sun* [Massachusetts] (6 May 1957).

11   Dorothy Roe (Associated Press Women's Editor), 'Being a Princess is Hard Work', *Syracuse Herald-American* (14 April 1957).

12   'Women Split on Sunglasses', *Syracuse Herald-Journal* (7 June 1957); 'Featured in Sunglasses', *Simpson's Daily Leader-Times* [Kittanning, Pennsylvania] (12 June 1957).

13   Eugenia Sheppard, 'Trend Back To Rimless Specs', *Winnipeg Free Press* (28 June 1962); Tad Rowady, 'Pretty Girls DoWear Glasses', *Daily Herald* [Tyrone, Pennsylvania] (20 February 1968).

14   Helen Howard, 'Why Women Wear Sunglasses', *Sunday Gleaner* [Kingston, Jamaica] (7 September 1969).

15   Rhoda Feldman, 'The Eyes Have It', *Winnipeg Free Press* (13 March 1980).

16   The oft-repeated story is that the 'Kelly' bag got its name and became popular after a magazine cover showed the pregnant Princess Grace using one to shield her stomach; the story does not seem to have appeared until the 1990s and no such cover appears to exist.

17   Madge Tivey-Faucon, 'Inside the Palace with Princess Grace', *Cosmopolitan* (March 1964), p.43.

18   United Press, 'Princess Grace Gives Millinery a Much-Needed Boost', *Berkshire Eagle* [Massachusetts] (1 February 1957); United Press, 'Princess Grace Honored', *Holland Evening Sentinel* [Michigan] (9 October 1957).

19   United Press, 'Princess Grace Reported Buying Maternity Dress', *Simpson's Daily Leader-Times* [Kittanning, Pennsylvania] (13 August 1957).

20   Eugene Gilbert, 'What Young People Think: Hero-Worshipping Teens Like Ike, Grace', *News-Tribune* [Fort Pierce, Florida] (13 October 1957).

21   Associated Press, 'London Paper Praises Grace', *Tucson Daily Citizen* (2 December 1957).

22   'Princess Will Wear Suits By Balenciaga', *New York Times* (21 November 1958).

23   William Glover, 'Grace Angry As Slipper Is Stepped On', *Cedar Rapids Gazette* (5 December 1958).

24   'The Princess and the Palace', *Look* (18 August 1959), p.56.

25   Pete Martin, 'I Call on Princess Grace', *Saturday Evening Post* (6 February 1960), pp.101–2.

26   Ibid., p.100.

27   Littlejohn, 'Princess Grace Tells Her Secrets'.

28   Martin, 'I Call on Princess Grace', p.101.

29   'The Princess and the Palace', *Look* (18 August 1959), p.56.

30   Pete Martin, 'I Call on Princess Grace', *Saturday Evening Post* (23 January 1960), p.42.

31   Jhan Robbins and June Robbins, 'The Pressures on Princess Grace', *Redbook* (November 1958), p.120.

32   Eugenia Sheppard, 'The Goddesses Meet', *Capital Times* [Madison, Wisconsin] (31 May 1961).

33   Winzola McLendon, 'Two Carolines Exchange Gifts', *Washington Post and Times Herald* (26 May 1961); Sheppard, 'The Goddesses Meet'.

34   Sheppard, 'The Goddesses Meet'.

35   Frances Levine, 'Jacqueline Kennedy Has Worldwide Acclaim of Fans', *Montana Standard-Post* [Butte] (23 July 1961).

36   'Reigning Beauties', *Time* (8 June 1962), p.30.

37   Geneviève Dariaux, *Elegance* (Garden City, New York, 1964), p.10.

38   Oleg Cassini, 'Fashion Secrets of Glamorous Women', *Kokomo Tribune* (13 October 1963).

39   Associated Press, 'Princess Grace Styles Blasted in London', *Reno Evening Gazette* [Nevada] (11 January 1963), quoting Jill Butterfield in the *Daily Express*.

40   'Fashion Focus on Monaco', *Charleston Daily Mail* [West Virginia] (30 January 1963); broadcast 17 February.

41   Eugenia Sheppard (Herald Tribune News Service), '008 Trails in Grace's Wake', *Washington Post and Times Herald* (19 May 1965).

42   Ibid.

43   'House of Dior Plans Lower-Price Clothes', *Des Moines Register* (31 December 1966). The dresses were designed by Phillippe Guiborge, Marc Bohan's assistant, and meant as a frivolity or *colifichet*.

44   Eugenia Sheppard, 'There's No But About It', *Syracuse Herald-American* (15 August 1965).

45   Louise Hickman (Associated Press), 'Mad Fashions Mark Paris Showing of Yves Saint-Laurent Openings', *Progress-Index* [Petersburg, Virginia] (8 August 1965).

46   Eileen Foley, 'Visiting Princess Grace Is Happy But Still Gets Homesick', *Daily Times-News* [Burlington, North Carolina] (23 September 1966).

47   'Three Are Named "Heads of Fame"', *Daily Review* [Hayward, California] (24 November 1968); the selection was made by the Helene Curtis Guild of Professional Beauticians.

48   Jean Sprain Wilson, 'It's Been 10 Years Since Grace Became a Princess', *Florence Morning News* [South Carolina] (10 April 1966).

49   Associated Press, 'Princess Grace Wins Fashion Sweepstakes', *Progress-Index* [Petersburg, Virginia] (16 June 1966), quoting Serena Sinclair in the *Daily Express*.

50   William B. Arthur, 'Princess Grace Turns Forty', *Look* (16 December 1969), p.100.

51   '2 Guests from Monaco in San Antonio Spotlight', *New York Times* (27 September 1968).

52   Muriel Davidson, 'What Princess Grace Likes and Doesn't Like About the Life She Leads', *Good Housekeeping* (January 1965), p.156.

53   Arthur, 'Princess Grace Turns Forty', p.99.

54   Eleanor Lambert, 'They're Hardly Baring Ankles', *Lowell Sun* [Massachusetts] (28 January 1970).

55   Curtis Bell Pepper, 'Her Serene Highness Princess Grace of Monaco', American *Vogue* (December 1971), p.176.

56   Enid Nemy (New York Times News Service), 'Ma Kelly Had a Lot of Influence', *Albuquerque Tribune* (30 April 1973); Arthur, 'Princess Grace Turns Forty', p.99.

57   Gillian Franks, 'Princess Grace has Aura of Serenity', *Winnipeg Free Press* (15 September 1970).

58   Yvette de la Fontaine (Women's News Service), 'Princess Brings Back Elegance', *Daily Times-News* [Burlington, North Carolina] (18 April 1968).

59   *Time* (28 March 1969), p.39.

60   Franks, 'Princess Grace has Aura of Serenity'.

61   Pepper, 'Her Serene Highness Princess Grace of Monaco', p.176.

62   Franks, 'Princess Grace has Aura of Serenity'.

63   Prudence Glynn, 'Princess Grace of Monaco: Perfect Typecasting', *The Times* (9 May 1972).

64   Franks, 'Princess Grace has Aura of Serenity'.

65   Glynn, 'Princess Grace of Monaco: Perfect Typecasting'.

66   Franks, 'Princess Grace has Aura of Serenity'.

67   Eugenia Sheppard, 'The Troubles of Being a Princess', *Washington Post and Times Herald* (15 August 1971).

68   Franks, 'Princess Grace has Aura of Serenity'.

69   'Looking Fantastic From Forty On: Princess Grace of Monaco', *Harper's Bazaar* (August 1975), p.55.

70   Douglas Keay, 'Life with Grace: An Exclusive Interview with Prince Rainier', *Ladies' Home Journal* (May 1974), p.167.

71   Stephen Birmingham, 'Princess Grace: The Fairy Tale 25 Years Later', *McCall's* (March 1981), p.147.

72   *Harper's Bazaar* (April 1978), p.85.

73   United Press, 'Princess Caroline at 18: A Serious Student, Casual Partygoer', *New York Times* (19 January 1975).

Acknowledgements

The publication of this book would not have been possible without the support of many people. First and foremost, we would like to thank HSH Prince Albert II of Monaco, both for authorizing the text and lending a collection of dresses from Princess Grace's wardrobe for the V&A exhibition *Grace Kelly: Style Icon* (17 April–26 September 2010). We are grateful to Van Cleef & Arpels for sponsoring the exhibition.

From the Princely Palace, Monaco, we thank Hervé Irien and Maryel Girardin and from the Grimaldi Forum, Sylvie Biancheri, Marc Rossi, Catherine Alestchenkoff, Christian Selvatico and Carl de Lencquesaing. They have all made this project a very enjoyable collaboration. We also received generous help from Evelyne Genta and Bérénice Würz at the Consulate General of Monaco in London, and from the Hon. Maguy Maccario Doyle, Elle Berdy and Karla Modolo of the Consulate General of Monaco in New York.

Many other individuals and institutions have provided assistance towards the book, the exhibition, or both. We are indebted to Philippe Le Moult, Soïzic Pfaff and Barbara Jeauffroy-Mairet at Christian Dior, Vanessa Guérin-Archambeaud at Yves Saint Laurent and Marie-Andrée Jouve; special thanks are due to Marc Bohan and Hubert de Givenchy for sharing their memories of Princess Grace, and Deborah Nadoolman Landis and Natasha Rubin for providing helpful information about costume design. Thanks are also due to the Executive Committee and Igor U. Zubizaretta of the Fundación Balenciaga, Getaria, Spain; William Doyle and Phil Donnelly of the Museum of Style Icons, Newbridge Silverware, Ireland; the Larry McQueen Film Costume Collection, Los Angeles; and Todd Fisher of the Debbie Reynolds Film Costume Collection, California, for lending dresses to the exhibition.

★ ★ ★

Jenny Lister would like to acknowledge the support of curatorial colleagues at the V&A including Oriole Cullen, Edwina Ehrman, Esther Ketskemety, Lesley Miller, Deirdre Murphy, Sonnet Stanfill, Suzanne Smith, Claire Wilcox, Christopher Wilk, Stephanie Wood and volunteers Carly Eck, Kay Manasseh and Laure Dalon. Victoria Broakes, Keith Lodwick and Geoff Marsh of the Theatre Collections have also provided extremely helpful advice. Particular thanks are due to Jo Ani, of the Development department, Rebecca Lim and Tina Manoli of the Exhibitions department, Lara Flecker and Sam Gatley of Textile Conservation, and the publishing team, including Mark Eastment, Head of V&A Publishing, copy-editor Delia Gaze and designer Damian Schober. Jenny Lister is also grateful to Mark Kilfoyle, Madeleine Ginsburg and the core team who created this book: Laura Potter, Samantha Safer and, most importantly, Kristina Haugland. She would also like to thank her family.

Kristina Haugland wishes to thank Jenny Lister and Laura Potter, who made transatlantic collaboration both possible and pleasurable. Her sincere appreciation goes once again to all at the Philadelphia Museum of Art who supported the research and production of her earlier publication *Grace Kelly: Icon of Style to Royal Bride,* including those in Publishing, Conservation, and the staff and volunteers of Costume and Textiles. She is deeply indebted to many friends and colleagues for their invaluable support, and will especially remain forever and fervently grateful for the life and love of Bill Gannotta.

Further Reading

Bradford, Sarah, *Princess Grace* (New York, 1984)

Cassini, Oleg, *In My Own Fashion* (New York, 1987)

Chierichetti, David, *Edith Head: The Life and Times of Hollywood's Celebrated Costume Designer* (New York, 2003)

Conant, Howell, *Remembering Grace* (New York, 2007)

Dherbier, Y.-B., and Verlhac, P.-H. (eds), *Grace Kelly: A Life in Pictures* (London, 2006)

Dufreigne, Jean-Pierre, *Hitchcock Style* (New York, 2004)

Dufresne, J.-L., Jeauffroy-Mairet, Barbara, and Leret, V., *Dior: les années bohan, 1961–1989: trois décennies de style et de stars* (Versailles, 2009)

Englund, Steven, *Princess Grace: An Interpretive Biography* (New York, 1984)

Haugland, H. Kristina, *Grace Kelly: Icon of Style to Royal Bride* (Philadelphia, 2006)

Head, Edith, and Calistro, P., *Edith Head's Hollywood* (New York, 1983)

Lacey, Robert, *Grace* (New York, 1994)

Mitterrand, F., and Meyer-Stabley, B., *The Grace Kelly Years: Princess of Monaco* (Milan, 2007)

Nadoolman Landis, Deborah, *Dressed: A Century of Hollywood Costume Design* (New York, 2007)

Quine, Judith Balaban, *The Bridesmaids: Grace Kelly, Princess of Monaco, and Six Intimate Friends* (New York, 1989)

Robyns, Gwen, *Princess Grace* (London, 1976, 1982)

Rose, Helen, *Just Make Them Beautiful: The Many Worlds of a Designing Woman* (California, 1976)
—, *The Glamorous World of Helen Rose* (Palm Springs, 1983)

Spoto, Donald, *The Dark Side of Genius: The Life of Alfred Hitchcock* (Boston, Massachusetts, 1983)
—, *High Society: Grace Kelly and Hollywood* (London, 2009)

Taraborelli, J. Randy, *Once Upon a Time: Behind the Fairy Tale of Princess Grace and Prince Rainier* (New York, 2003)

Picture Credits

Index